Organizing Solutions

for People with Attention Deficit Disorder

Organizing Solutions

for People with Attention Deficit Disorder

TIPS AND TOOLS TO HELP YOU TAKE CHARGE OF YOUR LIFE AND GET ORGANIZED

Susan C. Pinsky

A member of the National

Association of Professional

Organizers (NAPO)

FAIR WINDS
PRESS
GLOUCESTER, MASSACHUSETTS

Text © 2006 by Susan C. Pinsky

First published in the USA in 2006 by
Fair Winds Press, a member of
Quayside Publishing Group
33 Commercial Street
Gloucester, MA 01930

10 09 08 07 06 1 2 3 4 5

ISBN-13: 978-1-59223-234-2
ISBN-10: 1-59233-234-X

Library of Congress Cataloging-in-Publication Data available

Cover design by Yee Design
Book design by Yee Design

Photographer Credits
Courtesy of IKEA, www.ikea.com: 96, 120
Courtesy of Laura Ashley at prshots.com: 10, 112
Eric Roth: 130
Guillaume De Laubier: 72
Tria Giovan: 36, 66
Brian Vanden Brink, Photographer, Elliott Elliott Norelius Architecture: 106
Istock.com: 180

Printed and bound in Singapore

This book is dedicated to my husband, David Pinsky, whose love and support make everything possible.

Contents

Introduction

Early in my career as a professional organizer, I was hired by a vivacious and talented part-time artist whose home was among the messiest and most disorganized I had ever seen. We worked together one day a week to organize a space or set up an organizational system, but when I would return the next week, all would be undone. I would then have to waste valuable time re-addressing the old problems before we could move on to new ones. I could not, for the life of me, understand why this intelligent and capable artist had a harder time than most of my other clients maintaining the spaces and systems we had worked so hard to organize. Ironically, the answer to this question came from within my own family.

I came to the study of organizational solutions for people with Attention Deficit Disorder, or ADD, out of necessity rather than design. My eldest daughter was diagnosed with ADD when she was a fourth-grader. Up until that time, I had comforted myself with a series of excuses to explain away her difficulty managing her schedule and possessions. I alternately told myself that she was undisciplined, she was an "absent-minded professor" type, or our parental expectations were unreasonably high. But eventually it became clear that through no fault of ours or hers, my daughter struggled to stay focused on even the simplest of tasks.

A METHOD IS BORN

Not surprisingly, my jobs as a professional organizer and as the parent of an ADD-afflicted child soon began to overlap. Based on what I was learning about ADD, I was able to rely on my expertise as a professional organizer to weigh, adopt, reject, or modify organizational systems that could help my daughter. Conversely, my newfound knowledge of ADD led me to recognize that along with the aforementioned female artist, *many* of my chronically disorganized clients—and sometimes a client's chronically disorganized spouse or child— were exhibiting what I now know to be ADD behaviors and symptoms. I also discovered that the organizing systems I was using at home to assist my daughter were far more effective in the homes of these clients than the standard values, methods, and "tricks of the trade" I had previously used as a professional organizer. Over time, I was able to develop a clear methodology that responded to the specific needs of someone with ADD, and soon my client base drew heavily from that community.

If you have ADD and you struggle to stay organized, you may have asked yourself the following questions: How do I create an efficient life when the repetitive tasks required for good organization are too tedious to engage my attention, and when my possessions—even important and expensive ones—are constantly misplaced in moments of distraction? How do I live harmoniously with family members when my stuff tends to invade their space and my tardiness affects their schedules? These are discouraging questions, but based on years of work with countless ADD clients, I can assure you that good organizational skills are *not* beyond your reach. By re-examining some outdated values, simplifying your systems, refining your definition of organization, and adjusting some of your expectations, you *can* achieve a manageable and organized life.

This book is geared toward anyone whose life and home are affected by ADD, which includes both ADD sufferers *and* their frustrated family members striving unsuccessfully to keep an orderly home. It addresses those ADD symptoms that stand in the way of organizing—impulsivity, distractibility, perfectionism, memory lapses, and procrastination—but it also calls on the common strengths of ADD sufferers—enthusiasm, intelligence, ingenuity, and creativity—to aid in the search for a more organized life.

HOW TO USE THIS BOOK

This volume is divided into two distinct sections: Part I, "Organizing for the Disorganized," outlines my ADD-friendly organizing methodology, so you can apply it to your home, your schedule, and your life. It discusses the precepts and myths of good organization, and the reasons why some organizational strategies may be suitable for one individual with ADD, while others are disastrous. Part II, "Individual Projects," is arranged by room or project and consists of common, real-life organizing problems faced by my ADD clients and the solutions to those problems. These have been limited to mostly small-scale organizing tasks that won't overwhelm. While this book can be read from start to finish, it can also be used as a quick reference guide. Once you have finished reading Part I, feel free to flip ahead and find an organizational project that suits your needs. With each project you complete, my hope is that you'll have gained enough confidence in your organizing abilities to tackle yet another task until you're well on your way to a happy, harmonious, and more organized life.

PART 1

Organizing
for the Disorganized

In my work with ADD clients, I am often the third or fourth professional organizer to enter the home. Often my clients' bookshelves are teeming with volumes about organization, and their wallets are skinny from purchasing plastic tubs and drawer dividers, yet the house itself looks as though it has been transported to Oz via tornado. The visual chaos is often exacerbated by emotional turbulence within the home. Those members of the family who do not suffer from ADD cannot understand why the organizational systems they were at such pains to research, pay for, and set up are not being followed. They assume that the family member with ADD is lazy or inconsiderate, frustration leads to resentment, and tension follows.

Ironically, people with ADD do not tend to be lazy—they are instead some of the most energetic people I know, capable of boundless enthusiasm and dizzying creativity. What they are is discouraged, because the organizational systems that are handed to them are either so complex or so tedious that they are impossible for the ADD sufferer to maintain.

For someone with ADD, even the simplest task takes much more energy than it takes for others. To shower, get dressed, and get out the door in the morning can require the kind of care and concentration that average people expend over their entire day.

> **To set up a maintainable system for my ADD clients, I must first eliminate all of those systems that are too complex, unwieldy, and tedious and replace them with systems that are simple, fast, and convenient.**

> **The best organizational system for someone with ADD is the one that is most efficient, simplest, most convenient, and the easiest to maintain, because it requires the least number of steps and materials.**

The most difficult part of any job—getting started—has to be confronted and overcome multiple times for the ADD sufferer to accomplish even the most banal of tasks, like taking a shower. The attention-able need to overcome inertia and motivate themselves only once to begin their shower; people with ADD may have to motivate themselves four, five, or six times. They may start for the shower, only to find themselves back in the bedroom because they were distracted while fetching a clean towel from the hall linen cupboard; they may again start for the shower, only to end up in the kitchen, where they wandered after traipsing to the basement to rummage among the economy-sized supplies for a pack of soap bars. Again and again they must exercise the self-discipline to start for that shower, knowing full well that there is some chance they will again be frustratingly sidetracked. And while they expend this extraordinary mental energy to remotivate themselves, unshowered family members are probably berating them for laziness and lack of consideration. Is there any wonder that they are discouraged? Our ADD family member has been sabotaged by unnecessarily complicated, inconvenient, and tedious organizational systems (such as storing large supplies of common household items in the basement). Even relatively reasonable organizational systems that are workable for the rest of the family (such as storing towels in the hallway linen cupboard) may require an unreasonable amount of focus and effort for the ADD family member.

MAKE EFFICIENCY THE TOP PRIORITY

To set up a maintainable system for my ADD clients, I must first eliminate all of those systems that are too complex, unwieldy, and tedious and replace them with systems that are simple, fast, and convenient. Often my systems sacrifice beauty for efficiency. For instance, I might move a shelf into the bathroom to hold clean towels; I might position it next to the shower so that it can also hold shower support items such as shampoo and soap. This shelf might not match the bathroom decor—its open shelving with shampoo, razors, and soap bars visible might, in fact, *detract* from the decor—but it will enable the person with ADD to shower without having to take a series of inefficient side trips. Family members will then be empowered to *choose* between perfect aesthetics in the family bath or the chance at a timely shower.

Of course, floor plans, space, and routine vary widely from home to home. The solutions that work in one house may not be possible for another, but my greatest resource in adapting these systems is in fact the ADD client. People with ADD are fast thinkers—to paraphrase Dr. Edward M. Hallowell, author of *Driven to Distraction,* they have "Ferrari brains with Chevy brakes." It has also been speculated that because their minds race so quickly from one subject to another, they make connections through a kind of rapid-fire synthesis that eludes the rest of us. Once you give these "Ferrari" thinkers just a couple of ADD-appropriate tricks of the professional organizing trade, capture their interest, and put some of that formidable brainpower to work, there's no telling how far they will go in applying what they've learned in creative and effective ways. Let's start with the basic rules of organizing.

The single value that I most often have to convince clients to abandon in the name of efficiency is beauty.

While hidden storage solutions are sometimes more "beautiful," hooks and open shelving next to the shower provide an efficient support system for towels, razors, soaps, and shampoos.

The 14 Rules of Organizing

1. Give everything a home.

2. Store things on the wall or on a shelf, never on the floor.

3. Take advantage of vertical storage space by using tall shelves and bureaus.

4. Wherever possible, use hooks instead of hangers.

5. Don't increase your storage—reduce your inventory.

6. Touch it only once (file or toss mail as soon as you open it; don't add it to a pile you'll have to sort again later).

7. If you haven't used it in a year, discard it.

8. Duplicate where necessary to store things where you use them (toilet bowl brush in every bathroom).

9. Eliminate items that unnecessarily duplicate functions (hand can opener *or* electric can opener, not both).

10. Arrange your possessions within activity areas or zones.

11. Don't overcrowd shelving, cabinets, and drawers.

12. Make your things easy to access and easy to put away.

13. Name your cabinets and shelves (dish cabinet, sock drawer) to remind you that *only* these specific items are stored therein.

14. Make sure the "rough storage" areas in your home are well lit and easily accessible. Guard these areas well—they are more valuable than any other living area.

While these rules are a great foundation and will help guide you as you set out to change the way you live and organize, be sure to apply them only if they make sense in your situation. How do you know when it's okay to bend or break these rules? When they get in the way of efficiency.

Creating the Most Efficient System

In order to create this system, all other values must be subordinate to the interests of efficiency. I often walk into homes where clients have placed values such as beauty, frugality, or preparedness before efficiency. What they end up with is organized but inefficient—and for the ADD client, disastrously unmaintainable—systems. Remember this: Just because something is "organized" doesn't mean that it is efficient. Let me give an outrageous example: I could organize your shoes by putting all of your left shoes in the attic and all of your right shoes in the basement. Hey, it's organized. But it is neither efficient nor convenient; in the end, it requires too much effort to put on your shoes.

EFFICIENCY BEFORE BEAUTY

If you flip through this book, you will see some pictures of organized spaces that look like the "before" pictures in other organizing manuals. That is because other organizational systems are invested in beauty rather than efficiency. They would never show a picture of a bathroom with convenient, open shelving and shower supplies arranged haphazardly so they're easy to grab. It's just not as pretty to look at. The ADD client must be wary of those organizational systems that, although pretty, are neither practical nor sustainable.

While we can all enjoy the flawless charm of a meticulously organized space, we should not make the mistake of equating beauty with organization. Unfortunately, many people with ADD suffer from a kind of "perfectionism" (often tragically, frustratingly unattainable, given the nature of the disorder) that makes them quite vulnerable to this misguided yardstick of organizing success.

If I were to advise you, my ADD client, to sort your socks by mating them, rolling them, and then placing each pair in an individual bin, arranged by color (as a photo in a home goods catalog might encourage you to do), it's likely that the next time I visit your house, the bins will be empty, the socks will be in a half-

> Just because something is "organized" doesn't mean that it is efficient.

sorted pile on someone's bed, and you will be hopelessly discouraged. While mating, rolling, and placing in bins may be a sustainable organizing method for my other clients, my ADD clients need to employ a more efficient system. So to you, my ADD client, I would give the following advice: Identify a sock style of a medium weight, suitable for year-round use, and purchase two dozen in black and two dozen in white. Throw out all of your other socks. Allocate one bureau drawer to hold all of your socks and *only* your socks. Now you have achieved an organizational system for socks that is quick, easy, and practical. Socks need never again be mated and sorted. They get dumped directly and willy-nilly from the laundry into the sock drawer. Of course, the drawer will look like a wild jumble of white and black single socks (see photo on page 80), but for ADD clients, the goal cannot be beauty, it must instead be practicality.

Although this would be the most efficient sock system for the attention-able as well, they are at liberty to ignore it and pursue a less convenient but more aesthetically pleasing system. And while the person with ADD may occasionally put beauty before efficiency—she may in fact be a sock fashionista, who couldn't possibly limit herself to two types of socks—she will only be able to indulge her fetishes in one or two areas of her life.

For most of the systems in her home, the imperative must be efficiency. When an area becomes messy, the person with ADD must ask herself: has the number of my possessions been reduced enough, and my organizational system simplified enough, that it can be cleaned in a matter of minutes? Because for ADD clients, minutes may be all they have before the next beguiling, thoroughly captivating thought derails them from the task at hand.

SAVE YOUR SANITY, NOT YOUR MONEY

An efficient organizing system should save you time and space (not to mention stress), but I am sorry to say it will not necessarily save you money. In fact, frugality at the expense of time, space, and peace of mind can get in the way of an organized life. Every individual must find a personal balance between his finances and how much time and stress it costs him to accomplish his goals. But for the person with ADD, stinginess may be too expensive. In the sock example, I advised throwing out perfectly good socks and starting again with new socks. There was a price to be paid for efficiency, and that price came in the form of the loss of perfectly good socks and the retail value of several dozen pairs of replacement socks. But the time and effort saved on laundry day is worth that expense.

> Frugality at the expense of time, space, and peace of mind can get in the way of an organized life.

In the modern age, our society's rarest commodity is not goods, but time, and the ADD sufferer—who requires more time on average to complete a task—must guard his time as the most precious of all his possessions.

As it turns out, getting organized is one of the few problems in life you really can solve by throwing money at it. The key is to throw the money in the right direction, and to accept that services that may be an unnecessary expense for the attention-able are necessary and even therapeutic for you. If you have ADD, a lawn service, laundry service, or housekeeper may be essential to maintain your sanity and keep your life on track. I have clients who pay me simply to sit by their side for a couple of hours while they pay their bills. The knowledge that I am "on the clock" focuses their attention and urgency on bill paying; my presence in their schedule gives them the structure they require to get the job done. You may not need to hire a professional organizer, but I strongly recommend that, wherever possible, you procure a help-

> Saving money by buying sale items that you may or may not need, or will not need for a long time, is inefficient.

mate for larger tasks. Hire a neighborhood teenager to help you clean out your garage; working side by side with a more focused individual will help to keep you on task.

> For larger tasks, or tasks that regularly resist your efforts to complete, spending money to get help may well be the simplest, most convenient system.

Take Advantage of Your Family, without "Taking Advantage"

Family members may often be relied on to help out where professional assistance is unaffordable or unavailable. ADD children may require the presence of a parent in order to complete larger chores like bedroom cleaning. For adults with ADD, the spouse often provides an invaluable resource and helpmate for larger tasks around the home. Negotiating a trade of services with a family member or friend, rather than continuously asking for favors, may help to keep one partner from feeling used and the other from feeling burdensome.

Creativity and an intimate knowledge of your family members should allow you to come up with a task that you can take over for them in exchange for their organizing help. The ADD husband may, for example, solicit help with the garage by picking up an afternoon of childcare. Oil changes, dog walking, litter box maintenance, and toilet bowl cleaning can all be hard currency in The Great Family Bazaar. The trick is to enlist the attention and focus of the non-ADD family member for long jobs by trading a series of short—but possibly highly repulsive—jobs that are quick enough for you to successfully complete. If this is done right, all family members should come out of the trade feeling not just satisfied with their end of the bargain, but filled with the gratification that comes from making a good deal.

Procure the attention and focus of the non-ADD family member for long jobs by trading a series of short jobs that are quick enough for you to successfully complete.

STOCKPILING IS A SIN

The impulse buying habits of those with ADD combined with the bulk-buying obsession of our culture can easily lead to over-stressed storage areas and organizational Armageddon. Many of the ADD homes I organize are overflowing with reams of paper, silos of cereals, and, always it seems, crates of toilet paper. I often ask myself, what is the scope of this unfortunate digestive condition with which this family envisions becoming afflicted? To keep your household manageable, resist turning your valuable storage space into a warehouse bulk retailer. There's no need to store crates of items you don't yet need in your basement, especially when they will force out legitimate storage items that will then clutter your living areas. Also, it's just plan inefficient to make all those side trips carrying your giant purchases to the basement instead of the rooms where they'll be used. You may rationalize that this excess supply cuts down on trips to the grocery store and prepares you for a natural disaster, but all it really does is overwhelm your storage areas and add to the chaos in your home.

What's even worse than bulk shopping? A this-just-might-come-in-handy-some-day mentality. The ADD client will see a great sale for an item he doesn't need and assure himself that it is reasonable to buy this item because if he ever wants to do X, it just might come in handy, and who knows if he can ever find another. The desire to be prepared for an eventuality or activity that may or may not happen convinces the client he must take advantage of this opportunity. The only way to tackle disorganization and start fresh is to stick to the most efficient system, and preparing yourself for every possible eventuality is just too cumbersome.

To avoid overbuying, always go shopping with a list and practice strict adherence to the list. Limit purchasing to only those items for which you have an immediate need or use.

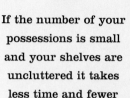

If the number of your possessions is small and your shelves are uncluttered it takes less time and fewer steps to find things and put things away.

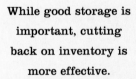

Buy only items for which you have an imminent plan or need.

While good storage is important, cutting back on inventory is more effective.

It's much better to rely on your ability to obtain things as you need them than to purchase reams of paper in case the stationery store is closed, a specialty saw because the local hardware store might not carry it, and a camping stove because it is cheap and you never know when you might want to take up camping. Saving money by buying sale items that you may or may not need, or will not need for a long time, is, well ... again, inefficient.

Buy only items for which you have an *imminent* plan or need. If you do someday have need of more, or something else, have faith that you are *already prepared* because you have the skills to procure it when you need it and the ingenuity to work around it if it can't be found.

MAKE PURGING A PRIORITY

The most efficient organizing system for someone with ADD requires a substantial reduction of materials. We have discussed how to keep things from entering your home; now we are going to address those things that are already in your home, because a house, closet, or garage that is stuffed with possessions will never be simple to use, efficient, or convenient.

My ADD clients seem to have a substantial and happy advantage over the general public when it comes to purging: They are often almost completely without closure issues. They have no emotional hang-ups surrounding letting go of their stuff, unlike the OCD (obsessive compulsive disorder) hoarders, the inveterate pack rats, and even your average clutter bug. People with ADD have been misplacing or breaking all of their most precious possessions since babyhood. They learned to let go and handle the disappointment back when they left their favorite toys to be stepped on and their blankies in parks and restaurants. They know from experience that you can live without most things and replace the rest. So encouraging someone with ADD to throw out mom's old electric fry pan is not a real challenge. That said, I still have a job to do with the ADD client, and it is merely this: I help him realize that he needs to reduce his inventory of perfectly good items and junk items alike, and that he should turn away from the excesses of our modern lives and, as much as possible, embrace a more spartan lifestyle.

How is getting rid of perfectly sound goods the most efficient system? It is more efficient because you are managing less stuff. If you reduce your number of dishes to the amount that will fill the dishwasher, then your sink won't fill with heaps of dirty dishes, and you won't be forced to move dirty dishes aside in order to use the sink. If you reduce the number of clothes, towels, and linens you own, you will have fewer piles of dirty and clean laundry hanging about the house, and less folding, sorting, and picking up to manage. If the number of your possessions is small, your shelves are uncluttered and it takes less time and fewer steps to find things and put things away. Yes, you will be forced to perform small jobs more often, rather than large jobs infrequently, but there is no net increase in work, just in the style of the work. And this frequent small job model is a more suitable system for those with ADD. You can get small jobs done, especially when you are motivated—and there is no better motivation than hunger to inspire one to wash a dish!

Although you may be comfortable culling some of your lesser-used and excess possessions, there will always be some rarely used items that you are hesitant to toss. While the general population can indulge themselves and hold on to these extras, it is imperative that people with ADD reduce as much of their unused possessions as possible. For this reason, try to adopt the following three philosophies:

1. Sentiment Is for Sissies

There is a value in holding on to items for sentimentality's sake. And many people with ADD derive comfort from familiar objects and routines. The problem arises when storage areas fill because too much is retained. Follow these guidelines to help you choose what to toss and what to keep.

Household Chores That Help You Purge

- **Putting away clean dishes.** If you have to shift items in your cabinet in order to fit your clean dishes, then go ahead and shift lesser-used and novelty items into the garbage can.

- **Doing laundry.** While folding laundry, fill a bag with rarely worn clothing suitable for donation and create a pile of slightly torn or soiled clothing to throw in the rag bin or trash.

- **Paying a bill.** When you pay bills, make sure there is a wastepaper basket within arm's reach. Most of the paperwork that comes into the house—including paid bills—can and should be filed in the wastepaper basket.

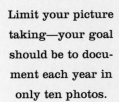

Limit your picture taking—your goal should be to document each year in only ten photos.

- Hold on to Grandma's favorite hankie, but get rid of her sleeper sofa.

- Keep baby's first outfit and antique christening gown, but get rid of your child's former favorite Mickey Mouse T-shirt, the sweater knitted by Grandma that he never wore, and the outfit he wore on the first day of school.

- Keep pictures that reveal family members' personalities and expressions; get rid of photos of people-less scenery and multiple pictures of family events. Two pictures of any birthday party are enough. One roll from any vacation is more than enough. Limit your picture taking— your goal should be to document each year in only ten photos. If you live to be eighty, that's a whopping 800 photos!

- If *you* can't use a hand-me-down or heirloom, or you don't like it, give it to someone who can or does. Mom's dining room set may be of excellent quality, and in seventy years it may be a valuable antique, but to store it for seventy years so that your grandchildren can see a small profit is an inefficient use of your space.

- Of your child's schoolwork, keep those items that are autobiographical—a drawing of "My Family" and essays entitled "What I'm going to do when I grow up," "My favorite things," and "My vacation." Get rid of the report on President Lincoln even if it got an A+.

- Of your child's artwork, keep two easily storable 8 x 11 works of art per year. When the child is eighteen, you can mount his art in a thirty-six-page photo album as a record and homage to his creativity. One album is charming, four boxes is pathological.

The bottom line is that you should keep anything that appeals to your taste and that you will use. If you like it but can't use it, or if you can use it but won't because you don't like it, get rid of it.

2. It's the Thought That Counts

Do you trust that it is the sentiment that has value and not the object itself? If so, then why are you hanging on to all of those gifts you don't like or can't use? You appreciated the sentiment when you said thank you—now get rid of all that stuff you don't want. Give it to charity so it can fulfill its destiny as a treasured item by finding its way into the home of someone who *will* treasure it.

If you feel that your friends or family members have too many closure issues regarding gift giving, if every gift is an obligation to be kept track of and "returned" to the giver when and if you can't use it, if you are worried that some boorish relative will ask, "Where is the thingamajig I gave you?" then you may wish to have a gentle conversation with them about the Protocols of Gift Giving that follow. There are only two, but they are immutable:

- **When you receive a gift, thank the giver. Once you've thanked the giver your obligations to the gift and the giver are over. If you like the gift, use it. If you don't like the gift, get rid of it. If you don't like the gift, but the giver is always around, use it once or twice and then quietly get rid of it.**

- **If you've been thanked, and know your gift has arrived, you must *never again* inquire about it. Do not tell the recipient to give it back to you if they can't use it. *You* gave it away, so you are not allowed to control its fate anymore; now *someone else* gets to decide what happens with it. Realistically, there will be some number of gifts for which the sentiment is greatly appreciated, but the object is not to the receiver's taste; it's unfair to put someone on the spot by making them confess that she doesn't like your taste, especially when she is in debt to you for a generous impulse.**

If there is only one boob in the family, and you don't see him often, it just may be easier to prepare a series of small white lies—"Oh, the dog knocked it over; I was heartbroken" or "I've put it away until the kids get older because I'm afraid it will get crushed." Don't feel guilty; it was bad manners for him to inquire in the first place.

3. Live in the Now

One of the largest barriers to getting rid of things is having an agenda for every item in your home. The decision to keep things for future use or resale value earns you little but the weighty burden of micromanagement. Although it seems financially responsible, it will probably instead cost you an organized and stress-free home. If you find yourself hesitating to get rid of something because you are holding on to it for your sister, waiting to get it appraised by a knowledgeable Hummel dealer, or planning to put it on eBay (after you get your digital camera fixed), then you are making it too complicated to reduce the inventory in your home.

If every time you go to purge, you worry that an item is worth something or too good to give to charity, then you suffer from the rag-picker syndrome. My great-grandfather was a rag picker by trade; he bought an old dress in one *shtetl* to tear up and sell for rags in the next. To engage in rag picking is to pursue a noble but time-consuming profession. But the question you must ask yourself is, is it *your* profession? Software engineers and full-time mothers don't have the time to take on the duties of an itinerant junkman, and someone with ADD certainly doesn't need another attention-sucking habit. It is both nobler and simpler to just donate all of your extra stuff to charity. (Ask for a receipt, and you can even claim it as a tax deduction!)

To reduce the amount of steps required to successfully purge your home of unused items, don't sell or dispose of your possessions in fifty places in fifty ways. Place anything that you are getting rid of in the front seat of your car, drop it at the Goodwill drop-off next time you are driving by, and then wallow in the twin satisfactions of an uncluttered home and a generous nature.

PURGE LIKE A PRO

Now that we have covered what *not* to keep, it's time to get down to business and start the purging process. Reducing your possessions down to a manageable number requires constant vigilance and liberal application of what I like to call The Brutal Purge.

During every organizing project, no matter how large (the garage) or small (a single kitchen cabinet), and every household chore (laundry, bedroom cleaning), purge with absolute abandon. In fact, if the only habit you change after reading this book is the adoption of The Brutal Purge, you will have gotten your money's worth.

Where Does It All Go?

There are three key destinations for your excess possessions: the trash, the curb, or a charitable organization.

If the object is of little value to others, throw it in the trash. If you think the object has some life left in it and you are fortunate enough to live on a busy street, placing objects on the curb with a "Free" sign can be an efficient method of de-cluttering your home. If not, application of The Brutal Purge requires that you find out where charities are located in your town. Goodwill and the Salvation Army take almost everything. Many grocery stores and shopping plazas have trailers or drop boxes for these charities or for old clothes. Make yourself as familiar with these drop boxes as possible. Once you know where you can drop off your stuff, you need only start moving it out of the house.

From here on out, you must not undertake an organizing or cleaning project without first setting out two bags (or boxes). These bags are designated as "trash" and "charity" respectively. At the end of the project, the trash bag goes to the trash can and the charity bag goes to the front seat of your car. This is very important: Items that are targeted for charitable donation but are left to linger on the shelf until you have time to "plan a trip" to the charity drop-off will be forgotten, and so will forever clutter your closets. Instead you want to clutter the front seat of your car. Every time you get in the car, you will think to yourself, "I have *got* to get this stuff out of the car. Is there any way I can plan my route so that I will go by the Salvation Army Trailer?" Putting the items in a prominent place in your car keeps them on

> Items that are targeted for charitable donation but are left to linger on the shelf until you have time to plan a trip to the charity drop-off will be forgotten, and so will forever clutter your closets.

your radar and provides the irritant that will motivate you to dispose of them. To maintain an organized life, moving possessions from the house to the car to the charity has to become a routine and regular errand.

MAKE USE OF STAGING AREAS

A staging area is a space in your home that is designated as a way station, an interim storage area, or an area devoted to short-term projects. The top of the stairs may be a way station for dirty dishtowels on their way down to the basement laundry. An empty shelf in the garage may host a bag of grub control to be spread on the lawn when the rain lets up. The dining room table may be temporarily covered with your latest crafting project materials. The rule of staging areas is that they're not pretty, but they *are* convenient and efficient.

Three Types of Staging Areas

Here are the three types of staging areas and the important functions they each serve:

1 **Way Station Staging Area:** Items in a way station staging area are actively in transit. This kind of staging area accommodates items that are either headed out the door or to their rightful place in the home. An effective way station must be in the direct path of the object's journey and should be so obvious, and even irritating, that you are motivated to move the item along. The front seat of the car, the doorknob on the garage door, and the floor in front of the garage door are all useful way station staging areas for getting things out of the house. The bottoms and tops of the stairs are equally important way station staging areas because dropping an item at the bottom of the stairs, so that you can scoop it up to put it away next time you go up the stairs, is just more efficient than running up and down the stairs ten times a day (which you won't do anyway).

The custom stair basket impedes the usefulness of this staging area. Beautified and hidden, items in the bottom of the basket will likely languish there for weeks.

Warning: *Do not use fancy baskets to beautify your staging area. These will merely hide the item you wish to put away, and of* *course, once it is beautified, hidden, and requires rummaging to locate at the bottom of a basket, you will no longer feel motivated to put it away.*

Top Five Way Station Staging Areas

- Front seat of the car
- Door handles
- The floor in front of your home's exits and entrances
- Top or bottom of a staircase
- Hallways and passageways

2 **Interim Staging Area:** Items in the interim storage staging areas need temporary storage until a specific date. An empty shelf in the garage, for example, might provide interim storage for the mosquito zapper that you purchased today but won't have time to set up in the yard until Sunday. An empty shelf in the basement may hold the troop camping equipment that you have been drafted to transport to next Thursday's Boy Scout Jamboree. Interim staging areas keep you from losing track of items that you will need in the near future and prevent unnecessary pileup of those items in the main living areas. Every rough storage area (basement, garage, attic) in your home should have empty shelving to create a buffer between clutter and your living areas. Do not worry that these shelves are "wasted" if they sit empty for much of the year. Empty shelves for interim storage are like the hammer in your toolbox. It stands ready to serve you, but like any tool, it won't necessarily get used every day.

> It is counterproductive to beautify a staging area—it is their very ugliness that makes them so useful.

Top Five Interim Staging Areas

- The trunk of the car
- The garage
- The front and back hall closets
- The basement
- The attic

3 Project Staging Area: Your desktop and the kitchen counter, where you already work on short projects like bill paying and cooking and then clear the surface and start again, are both useful project staging areas. For more involved projects (like sewing, scrapbooking, financial planning, etc.) that you want to leave out for several days, set up a folding table in the basement as a project staging area or employ a seldom-used dining room table. The right short-term project staging areas can help those with ADD keep their paints, pastels, graphics, and paperwork off the kitchen table and away from the family room couch.

Top Five Project Staging Areas

- The food prep counter
- Your desktop
- The dining room table
- The workbench
- Ancillary support surfaces, such as a table in the office

Project staging areas will work for you, not against you, if you commit to using them for only one project at a time.

The Tools of Organization

Having urged you to hire help and donate rather than sell or consign unwanted possessions, I am relieved to be able to tell you that organizing your space does not require expensive purchases. You don't need custom closets and fancy garage systems. Most everything you need to organize your home can be bought at discount department stores and hardware stores, and with the exception of cheap finished shelving (schedule a good hour), everything can be assembled or installed in less than fifteen minutes.

On the other hand, if your house is underfurnished, you may need to buy bureaus, breakfronts, and bookcases to create a reasonable amount of storage space for your possessions. But with a reduction of possessions (The Brutal Purge), even your furniture requirements may be more modest than you think.

HANGING TOOLS

A hammer, nails to hang things on, and the occasional screwdriver for putting up fancier hooks, with few exceptions, are just about the sum total of tools you will need to create an efficient system for hanging towels, coats, necklaces, calendars, rakes, brooms, and more. Good storage should be easy to set up and flexible, and nothing is more simple, cheap, and flexible than a hammer and nail.

SHELVING TOOLS

I regularly urge my ADD clients to procure these same organizational tools: modular plastic shelves for the garage and basement and cheap, tall open finished shelves for in the house.

Rely on tall open shelving for the bulk of your storage needs—the easiest method for putting something away is to pop it onto a shelf; if you have to open cupboard doors or pry off lids, you've added an unnecessary step, which is an impediment to putting things away. Limit your inventory to a reasonable number, and your shelves will remain uncluttered and easy to use and your storage needs will not be too expensive.

> Good storage should be easy to set up and flexible, and nothing is more simple, cheap, and flexible than a hammer and nail.

> Open shelving is an invaluable ADD organizing tool because it allows you to put things away in one easy step.

Sturdy modular plastic shelving takes advantage of vertical storage space and can be assembled in ten minutes with a rubber mallet.

If necessary, pay a handy man to assemble cheap pre-finished shelving—available at any discount store—for efficient storage in the living areas of your home.

TUBS AND BINS

Almost any area in your home—basement, garage, playroom—can be organized by procuring tall, cheap shelving and using lidless, clear plastic tubs (lids prevent you from being able to "wing" things in) or open-front stacking bins to corral items on the shelves.

Clear plastic tubs without lids are useful for storing small collections from dishtowels to Barbies. If your tub comes with a lid, leave it off, toss it out, or store it beneath the tub. (For storage in very dusty areas, simply rest the lid on top as a dust guard, without actually snapping it on.) Make sure to choose clear tubs; you shouldn't have to touch it to know what's inside, and you certainly don't want to waste time managing labels.

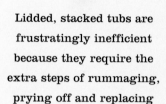

Lidded, stacked tubs are frustratingly inefficient because they require the extra steps of rummaging, prying off and replacing lids, and restacking to procure or retrieve an item.

Clear open plastic tubs on shelves are very convenient. Do not stack or use lids —it only impedes access to the items stored inside. The larger tub in this image has an attached lid that hangs down and out of the way; this is a comforting style for those who object to throwing out the lids.

If you must use lidded or opaque tubs, do yourself a favor and *do not* stack them. Lidded, stacked tubs are horribly inefficient because they require the extra steps of rummaging, prying off and replacing lids, and restacking, to procure or retrieve an item. Opaque tubs are particularly bad for stacking because anything inside goes "off your radar." It requires too much effort and shifting to remind yourself what is stored in which, or to access anything on the bottom, so the contents are rarely if ever used again—you might as well just put your possessions in the trash.

Open front bins on shelves are the most efficient container system. Items stored inside are easy to access and easy to put away. This bin has a solid bottom so smaller items won't slip out.

An open-front stacking bin with a low lip is another great organizing tool, because everything inside is easy to access and a breeze to put away.

I generally discourage stacking and instead recommend these bins as an alternative to tubs on open shelving. But because these bins are open in front, they are appropriate, if necessary, for stacking.

Make sure the bins are oriented so that the open side is the longer side—you want them wide, not deep, in order to promote ease of access. Avoid wire-style bins, as small pieces can fall through the mesh. A solid bottom is best.

THE IMPORTANCE OF ROUGH STORAGE

It is essential for someone with ADD to conserve as much rough storage space as possible. Resist the common practice of "finishing" the *entire* basement. You probably already have a family room, an underused living room, and a never-used dining room. An oversized living area will not compensate for the loss of rough storage space for athletic equipment, camping equipment, tools, and seasonal storage. When rough storage is eliminated, these items are forced to find refuge in overstuffed closets and beleaguered garages. It then becomes burdensome, time-consuming, and overwhelming to access or put away those items that *legitimately* belong in the closet or garage, and so, of course, nothing is ever put away. Guard your rough storage areas—they have a price above rubies, for they are your only defense against distracting and inefficient clutter in your living spaces, and additional and inefficient steps in future projects.

Guard your rough storage areas—they have a price above rubies, for they are your only defense against distracting and inefficient clutter in your living spaces.

The ADD Organizing Method

You have been given a list of the tricks of the organizing trade; you have been educated in the myths of organizing; you have eschewed those values that are inappropriate for someone with ADD; you have been given a doctrine—Efficiency—from which to judge all organizational systems; and you have been given a list of practices, physical spaces, and tools that will help in your quest for greater organization. All that remains is a step-by-step procedural template that you can employ for every project in which you organize a space—be it large (the garage) or small (a single kitchen cabinet). All organizational projects require the following approach:

SIMPLE STEPS FOR ORGANIZING A SPACE

1 **Prepare.** Find your local charities and drop boxes, and call your town or waste management company to discover pick-up dates for large items or hazardous waste.

2 **Set up.** Put out two containers—one for charity and one for trash. Designate spots for "other area" items that belong in other areas of your home, like a "goes upstairs" pile or a "belongs in basement" pile. Designate areas for categories of items that will be returned to the about-to-be organized space; in a garage, this might mean an "athletics equipment pile," "landscape pile," or "auto support pile."

3 **Clear.** Empty the space (garage, cabinet, etc.) of all items, sorting them into the various "keep" piles, "other area" piles, charity pile, and trash pile. Be sure to weed out and purge the unused, unwanted, unliked, soiled, and spoiled, along with duplicates, novelty items, and too-difficult-to-store items.

4 **Clean.** Clean out the space (wash down the interior of the cabinet, sweep out the garage, etc.).

5 **Name.** Name the space and designate areas within the space. The garage might have a landscaping shelving unit and an auto support shelf; a china cabinet might have a plate shelf and a mug shelf.

6 **Reduce.** Identify those items in the "keep" piles that no longer belong in the space (cook pots that don't belong in the china cabinet, for example), and put those things in the appropriate "other areas" piles. Cast your eye over your "keep" pile and judge whether it will comfortably fit in the space. If not, remove more items for charity.

7 **Procure.** Procure appropriate storage tools (nails on which to hang rake handles, modular shelves on which to stack gardening supplies, etc.) and place in the space.

8 **Return.** Return *appropriate* items and *only* appropriate items (complies with the name) to the space. Be careful not to overcrowd, stack, or otherwise render items inaccessible.

9 **Put away and clear away.** Put away the items in the "other areas" piles (hopefully one trip per area); take trash to the garbage; put donations in the front seat of the car.

10 **Bask.** You've worked hard; give yourself a moment to admire your newly organized space.

This is the simple procedure for organizing every room, closet, and cubby in your home. You can use it as a guide to organize any space not covered in this book. However, on larger projects, or for those chores that are regularly neglected, you might consider hiring a professional or working with someone in your family.

Great Expectations

It's important that you give each organizing project your all, but that you also maintain realistic expectations. Do not expect that after reading this book and applying these techniques, your house will be miraculously transformed into a Martha Stewart dream home or that your life will be void of the colorful escapades, misplaced objects, and hair-raising timing that are part and parcel of life with ADD. What can be expected is that when your home is messy, that mess will be only one layer deep, and you'll know how to fix it.

The delightful whirlwind that is you will and should still be evident in both your surroundings and your day. But if you apply the systems and techniques I recommend and simplify the task of organizing, you'll reduce the clutter in your space to a level that is both manageable and comfortable.

Creating Work Spaces That Work for You

An efficient work space is a powerful tool for keeping yourself organized. Your work spaces could include everything from an office to a home carpentry shop. They are a subset of activity areas that should be outfitted with storage and space enough to pursue your work and store all the support items necessary to that work.

Know your limits and work habits. Do you work better with music? Then have support systems (like a CD player) for music in your office. If extraneous noise is too distracting to you, then create a bare-bones, distraction-free work space that allows you to hyper focus. Depending on your style, shiny things to touch and fondle might provide needed distractions or be too distracting—plan accordingly. Do you need a place to pace? Then keep a path clear. Do you think better in a rocking chair? Then get one. The more you question yourself to explore the distractions that keep you from working, as well as the tools that help you focus, the more organized and productive you will become.

PART II

Individual Projects

CHAPTER 1

The Kitchen

For those with ADD, the kitchen may seem like the ultimate foe. You feel like you can never keep up with the dirty dishes, the crumbs on the counters, and the piles of mail that seem to invade this room. The key to slaying this monster is to break up your organizational process into smaller, more gratifying projects. It's okay if you can't make the kitchen spotless in one attempt. Little by little, you can chip away at it. Remember, the kitchen doesn't need to look beautiful and perfect all of the time. But in order for you to maintain peace of mind and relieve stress, it does need to be organized enough to find what you need. This chapter addresses some common kitchen problems and then guides you through some quick and easy projects to get that kitchen organized. As you start the kitchen re-organization process, keep the following Kitchen Organizing Commandments in mind:

KITCHEN ORGANIZING COMMANDMENTS

- Use your kitchen for cooking only.
- Designate and name areas for each activity.
- Segregate activities and their associated tools into designated areas.
- Do not over-shop; buy only those items that are on your shopping list and for which you have imminent plans.
- Do not overstock; get rid of old, unused, excess, and novelty cookware, china, and foods.
- Locate china and cookware, not food, in areas that are convenient to the sink and dishwasher.

Paper Pileup

PROBLEM

"My kitchen is always buried under a pile of papers."

SOLUTION

Food and papers don't mix. There is nothing more disabling than a mixture of papers and dishes cluttering the kitchen. The simplest and best organizational plan is to ban all paperwork from the kitchen. It's just easier to keep a kitchen organized if you use it only for cooking, and not for crafts or office work. If you must have a kitchen office, then segregate the office from the kitchen supplies. Name one cabinet and counter "The Kitchen Office"— try to choose an area near the kitchen phone. Then remove all kitchen supplies (food/dishes) from this space and replace them with office support items (paper, pen, stacking trays, and most important, a trash can). Keep your papers corralled in your new office space apart from food and dishes, and keep food and cookware away from your designated office area.

If you keep to this rule, you will greatly improve your life. Kitchen cleanup will not overwhelm if it doesn't include organizing the paperwork, and paper organization will be less daunting if it doesn't include cleaning the kitchen. By maintaining strictly separate spaces for food prep and paperwork, you will have gone a long way toward dividing and conquering both your kitchen and office organizational challenges.

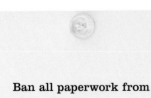

Ban all paperwork from the kitchen.

To keep the daily newspaper from cluttering kitchen counters, place a paper-recycling bin somewhere in your kitchen where you can easily toss the day's newspaper once you have perused it.

Kitchen Cabinet Clutter

PROBLEM

"I can never seem to get my kitchen cabinets organized."

SOLUTION

People with ADD tend to be more impulsive, which leads to over-shopping and results in overcrowded cabinets filled with unnecessary items. The best way to solve this problem in the future is to commit to strict adherence to the grocery list. To repair damage already done, you must perform The Brutal Purge. Make room for the stuff you do use by getting rid of the things you don't. When is the last time as a single male that you used that Bundt pan? Do you ever plan on eating that cherry raisin oatmeal? Donate kitchen items that are not versatile or don't store well. That huge fish-shaped platter that doesn't nest and that decorative porcelain pie dish with molded apples sticking out of its lid are both ripe for donation. Get rid of duplicates. When is the last time you used all four of those casserole dishes *at one meal*? After you throw out, donate, or consign these excesses, your cupboards will be roomy, spare, and much easier to keep organized.

Clear up extra cabinet space by getting rid of odd-shaped dishware and specialty cookware.

Tupperware TNT

PROBLEM

Too much inventory, precarious stacks of yogurt tubs, nested containers, and lids stored separate from tubs, make this an inefficient, cluttered cabinet.

"Every time I take out or put away Tupperware, the cabinet just seems to explode and a cascade of Tupperware comes tumbling down."

SOLUTION

Storing lids on their containers and stacking only like-sized containers allows retrieval and storage in one simple motion. More importantly, reducing the containers to a reasonable number eliminates the stress and clutter.

Defusing the Tupperware bomb requires that you reduce your Tupperware stock to a number that is just shy of what you think you need. It is inefficient to be constantly rifling through and organizing scads of Tupperware when you need only a handful of pieces. The typical family of five should own one set of Tupperware containing a *maximum* of five pieces (smaller families should own even less!). It is unlikely that you would ever need to use more than this number at any one time. The final goal should be not merely to comfortably fit the *appropriate amount* of Tupperware neatly and conveniently into your cabinets, but to *make sure* that you run short on Thanksgiving. It is more efficient to use a ziplock bag and some tinfoil once in a while than to clutter the cabinets with enough Tupperware to see you through the overland route to China.

Tupperware Tips

1 **Avoid nesting your Tupperware.** It is just too much hassle to take out and put away nested pieces. Instead put the pieces next to each other, or stack those that are the same size. Store each piece with the lid on it—eliminating the need to hunt for matching lids—as this is absolutely the most convenient and efficient method for storing and retrieving.

2 **Use Tupperware for food prep and serving dishes.** When used in a way that saves you steps, Tupperware can be very ADD-friendly. For example, making tuna fish salad in a Tupperware container will save you from having to wash a bowl and allows you to keep leftovers where they are. Serving fruit salad in a Tupperware bowl saves you the trouble of transferring it to a serving dish, which would later need to be washed. (Transversely, if you serve a casserole in a china dish, you can avoid transferring leftovers to Tupperware by using plastic wrap or tinfoil.)

3 **Do not use Tupperware to store cereal and other packaged goods.** When used in a way that creates unnecessary extra steps, Tupperware becomes your enemy. For example, transferring your Cheerios to Tupperware containers when it already comes in a perfectly good box is a waste of time and energy. Do you really have all this extra attention to spend on repackaging all of your groceries? And are you planning to label each Tupperware with the appropriate expiration date every time you make this transfer? For Heaven's sake, I'm exhausted just thinking about it!

Steps to Tupperware Reduction

1 Reduce your Tupperware inventory to five pieces or fewer.

2 Throw out *all* of Tupperware's poor second cousins—old yogurt containers, butter tubs, etc.

3 On garbage day, throw out the contents of all the Tupperware containers in the fridge.

Which Tupperware to Keep

In choosing which Tupperware pieces to keep or acquire for optimum sensible storage, remember that your Tupperware should be:

- **Clear.** This allows you to see what's in it.

- **Square or rectangular (not both).** Having pieces with the same shape means they will stack, and squared corners will fit more efficiently in fridges and cabinets.

- **Untapered.** This allows you to get more storage space for the same footprint.

Spice Rack Dilemma

PROBLEM

Spice storage is inefficiently divided between a deep cabinet that obscures all but the front row of spices and a hard-to-maintain decorative rack.

"I can never find the spice I want to use, and my spice rack is a jumbled mess."

SOLUTION

Inventory has been reduced, all spices regardless of size or packaging are visible, spices are loosely alphabetized, and empty shelving is maintained.

Make visibility your first priority, so that you remove only the spice you need; someone with ADD shouldn't have the burden of rearranging her spices every time she makes a meal. Visibility is achieved through reduction and improved access. Ask yourself the following questions: Are most of my spices invisible because they live in a deep cabinet where only the front layer can be seen? Has it been more than two years since I culled out spices that are more than a year old? (Eeewww.) Am I holding onto obscure spices purchased for failed recipes that will probably not be used again? Are my spices inconveniently divided between my cupboard and a decorative spice rack? Am I organizing them in little categories such as "savory" and "sweet"?

If you answered yes to these questions, start by throwing out those decorative spice racks. It just takes too many steps to transfer your spices into pretty uniform jars; you lose any sense of the age of the spice; and your spice collection will never perfectly conform to the labels on the rack. Many of these racks also make it difficult to put spices away; the "lazy Susan" spinning style is particularly egregious. Instead, identify a space near the food prep area where you can install the simple wire-shelf-style spice racks available at any container store. Many of these do not need screws but merely clip over a door or cabinet door. Gourmet cooks with larger inventories may need two racks installed on both doors of a double door cabinet. This rack should have the depth for a single jar or tin only. (Gone are the days of storing spices in front of each other!) Purge old, unwanted, and rarely used spices, and arrange your remaining spices in a single row in loose alphabetical order, leaving a little extra space on the shelf.

Spice Sense

- Throw away any spice that hasn't been used in a year.

- Get rid of decorative spice racks and install a simple, shallow, shelf-style rack large enough to comfortably hold all of your remaining spices with space left over. (Gourmet cooks may need to use two racks or a longer rack that runs the height of a door.)

- Loosely alphabetize the remaining spices.

- Place spices side by side in a single row so that all are visible.

Whenever possible, buy fresh spices; many grocery stores now sell them in small packets. Yes, they are expensive and you may not use all of them, but they taste better and will help you keep spice clutter at bay.

A Surplus of Small Appliances

PROBLEM

"I don't have room to store all my small appliances, but I do plan on using them one day, so I'd hate to get rid of them."

SOLUTION

Grand dreams of gourmet meals may once have led you to immoderate shopping, but it's misplaced sentiment, obligation, and guilt that make you keep the clutter. Dump the stuff and drop the guilt. If you have spent scads of money on espresso machines, coffee presses, and waffle irons that you've used once and then abandoned, if these behemoths are cluttering your kitchen while chastising you with silent recriminations, then it is time to recalculate their cost in the currency of stress and space.

If a small appliance is rarely used, is broken, or duplicates the function of another tool, then get rid of it. Ask yourself, "Do I need *both* a toaster and a toaster oven? Both a manual and an electric can opener? Do I in fact prefer a good old-fashioned sharp knife to an electric knife? And do I really appreciate my coffee that much more if I grind it myself?" Once you begin to honestly answer these questions, you'll be able to free up a lot of useful space in your cabinets and on your kitchen counters.

Simple Rules for Small Appliances

- Look over your small appliances and get rid of anything that you do not *currently,* regularly use, no matter what it originally cost you. If it hasn't been used in more than a year, out it goes.

- Identify small appliances that duplicate the functions of other tools and then eliminate any redundancies.

- Be wary of impulse gadget purchases. Many small appliances are not used often enough, or their functions are not appreciated enough, to justify the amount of counter and cabinet space they require.

- Rely on fresh ingredients; gourmet meals are the result of perfectly ripened produce, not small appliances.

Knife Control

PROBLEM

"I have lots of knives, but I use only a few of them because it's hard to find time to sharpen the others."

SOLUTION

Get rid of those dull, old, and unused knives—accept that you are never going to have the time to take on the duties of a cutler. Reduce your knife collection to your few remaining sharp knives. Chef Anthony Bourdain, author of *Kitchen Confidential,* admonishes us to procure one good knife and be done with it: "Please believe me, here's all you will need in the kitchen department: *one* good chef's knife, as large as is comfortable in your hand." No doubt Mr. Bourdain is correct, but one or two small paring knives and a large blunt-nosed serrated knife—available for three dollars at any grocery store—can also come in handy. Pare your knife collection down to the four or five knives that are sharp and that you use most frequently. Do not then leave these fortunate and useful few to rattle around threatening bodily harm with every blind reach into the cutlery drawer; instead store them in a drawer knife block. I prefer drawer knife blocks to countertop knife blocks because even with the extra step of opening the drawer, it takes less effort to slide a knife into a long slot open on the top than to stab it from the side into a tiny hole.

A magnetic strip that is screwed into the wall near the food prep area is a convenient knife storage method. If you have the wall space, are handy with a screwdriver, and don't have young children in the home, then this is your most efficient option.

Unruly Cooking Utensils

PROBLEM

Duplicates, novelty purchases, hidden knives and "intruders" make this drawer inefficient and even dangerous.

"My cooking utensils always seem to be in a disorganized jumble in my kitchen drawers."

SOLUTION

Thanks to a reduction of inventory and the use of a knife block, the most oft used utensils can be plucked from this tall canister in one efficient motion.

Cooking utensils must have their own home, all to themselves, near the sink. Start your organizing project by evicting any intruders (rubber bands, pens, etc.) from your cooking utensils' current home. Next, go through your utensils and eliminate duplicates, rarely-to-never-used items, and impulse purchases. How many wooden spoons do you really need? (Answer: one. I know it might be dirty when you need to use it, but don't you have a sink?) Do you need all of those old, chewed-up spatulas? Are you likely to use that candy thermometer again?

Now that you have pared down your possessions, consider storing your utensils in something other than a drawer. Too many utensils in a drawer fit awkwardly, bunching up and rattling, so the drawer itself is difficult to open because the ladle is having relations with the potato masher. Store them instead in a carousel or large "jar" (glass, ceramic, or metal) so that you can see everything you have without having to open a drawer. It is also more efficient to drop clean cooking utensils in a carousel or jar than to wrestle with a stuck drawer. If you decide to use a jar, put your most oft-used items in the jar and leave the lesser-used items in the now roomy drawer.

Easy Utensil Organizing

- Remove "intruders" from your cooking utensil storage area.

- Get rid of duplicates and rarely used novelty pieces.

- Store all, or your most often used, cooking utensils in a carousel or jar.

Pot Patrol

PROBLEM

"Even though I nest, I have trouble fitting all my pots and pans in my cabinets."

SOLUTION

Limiting inventory to four pots allows for easy storage—no rummaging or nesting required.

Consider replacing your cook pots with attractive enameled **covered** pots that match or coordinate with your dishware. Because they can be used for cooking, serving, and storing soups, sauces, casseroles, and cooked veggies, they save you from dirtying other dishes!

Reduce your collection to four to six of your most often used pots, and I guarantee that pot storage will immediately become simpler. Those inefficient extra steps of shifting and nesting take unnecessary time and effort. Most households can get by with one fry pan, one saucepan, and two large cook pots. If you are an omelet lover or Chinese food lover, you may add an omelet pan or wok to your collection, but refrain from keeping too many specialized pots. On Thanksgiving, you can always supplement your cookware with a disposable roasting pan.

If you have culled your collection down to four, it should not pose much of a problem to find a cabinet (be sure to banish everything but cook pots from this cabinet) where all of your pots can fit side by side, no pan in front of or blocking another, and no pot stacked on another. Storing your cook pots un-nested, side by side, will also allow you to store pot lids directly on the pots— a method that will forever simplify your life. If your cabinet is so small that you must nest, then screw a small hook into the side of the cabinet and hang the extra lid or two by their rims.

Pot Protocol

- Designate a large cabinet near the sink for pots.

- Eliminate specialty pots and reduce your pot collection to no more than four to six pots.

- Store your pots so that no one pot blocks another and, if possible, avoid nesting.

- If you must nest, screw small hooks into the side of your pot cabinet and hang the pot lids from them.

- Replace the majority of your pots with attractively enameled covered cookware that can double as serving and storing pieces.

Food Cabinet Follies

PROBLEM

SOLUTION

Overcrowding, and a failure to name this cabinet makes it hard, not only to find a particular item, but also to decide which items belong.

"I forget what I have on hand and buy the same groceries twice, so my cabinets are packed to the limit."

Reducing the inventory, stacking identical items only, and leaving empty shelf space make it easy to store and retrieve food items. Naming the shelves—from top to bottom "snacks," "breakfast" and "cans"—gives you a guide for which groceries and how many, can be appropriately stored here.

Stop keeping a large stock of groceries "on hand"; reduce your food inventory to those foods you have imminent plans to eat, then stick to your shopping list so that you purchase only the groceries needed for the next few days' menu plans.

The most common culprit in food cabinet clutter is food you have no plans of ever eating due to its old age or lack of appeal, or food that you don't end up eating because it was purchased outside of a menu plan. Tossing out all this food at once is too overwhelming, but you should have no trouble organizing your cupboards one at a time over the course of several days.

Use the cabinets farthest from your sink to store food. Maintain your clutter-free cabinets by suppressing the common tendency to hoard enough food to get you through a nuclear winter; after all, you probably live within easy driving distance of a grocery store. Make sure that your cabinets always retain empty shelf space. Maintaining open space will make putting away groceries a one-step task, appropriate for someone with ADD. Be guided by the following rule: If a cabinet no longer has empty shelf space for groceries, then it is time to make some donations to the food pantry and garbage can.

Food Cabinet Rules

1 Never buy anything that you aren't actively planning to eat in the coming week.

2 Avoid impulse shopping by purchasing only those items noted on the running grocery list (on the pad and paper you keep in the kitchen specifically for this purpose).

3 Don't allow your cabinets to fill up; maintain empty shelf space.

Be guided by the following rule: If a cabinet no longer has empty shelf space for groceries, then it is time to make some donations to the food pantry and garbage can.

Food Cabinet Follies, continued

Food Cabinet Cleanup

Here's an easy way to organize a single food cabinet:

1 Empty the food cabinet and clean the interior.

2 Sort through the contents and eliminate old or novelty food items.

3 Cast your eye over the remaining food and divide the food as best as you can into as many categories as you have empty shelves.

4 Name the empty cupboard shelves after those categories. For instance, one shelf might be called Snacks, another will be Breakfast, and a third will be Canned Goods. Now return only the snacks, cereals, and canned goods to the cabinet, being sure to segregate them to their respective shelves.

5 Do a quick survey of the other kitchen cabinets to move snacks, cereals, and canned goods found elsewhere into their new permanent home. Check expiration dates and apply the six-month rule (tossing out items you haven't touched in six months) so that you do not litter your newly organized cabinet with The Old, The Novelties, and The Mistakenly Acquired.

6 Place all of the food that was formerly housed in the newly organized cabinet, and that does not now adhere to the cabinet's new designation, in a more appropriate cupboard.

7 Take out the garbage and, if applicable, put your food pantry donation bag in the car or in front of the door to the car.

8 Repeat these steps at intervals until all the cabinets are organized.

Brown Paper Bag Storage

Store all brown paper shopping bags in the paper recycling bin. If you need to get ahold of one or two, you will know where to find them, and in the meantime, you won't waste valuable kitchen cabinet space storing your garbage. If your town does not provide for paper recycling, then it is acceptable to keep three or four bags folded and slipped sideways onto a shelf in a tall, slender cardboard box. Imagine a tall, boxed set of three or four books—this is the look you are going for. The box will corral your bags, keep them neat, and give you a guide for how many you can keep; once your slender box is full, throw out any new bags. As for those of you who feel you need more than three or four bags, I ask you, when is the last time you needed half a dozen brown paper bags, and if you did need them, wouldn't you know where to get more?

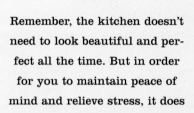

Remember, the kitchen doesn't need to look beautiful and perfect all the time. But in order for you to maintain peace of mind and relieve stress, it does need to be organized enough to find what you need.

Plastic Shopping Bag Storage

More than brown paper bags, plastic grocery bags and shopping bags are a common pest in many kitchens. The best way to tame that bothersome surplus of plastic bags is to throw most of them out immediately after unpacking the shopping. Shove the rest in a canvas bag, hung by one handle from a nail. Never allow the canvas bag to fill—you don't want it to start spewing plastic. Once it is half filled, throw out all new plastic grocery bags. As for those nice handled shopping bags that you get from department stores and boutiques: Keep one with the brown paper bags, and then, no matter how beautiful, throw the rest out.

Dish Cabinets of the Damned

PROBLEM

To remove anything from, or restore anything to, this cabinet requires rummaging and re-arranging graded towers of nesting dishes.

"Our dishes are precariously piled in the cabinet and threaten to topple over because my ADD wife places them there haphazardly."

SOLUTION

The shelves have been named "serving bowls," "bowls/glasses" and "plates" and all other items have been removed. Excess dishware was eliminated. Dishes are stacked rather than nested allowing for the removal or replacement of a dish in one efficient motion.

Reduce the dishes in your cupboard to a number that can be stored without rummaging, shifting, and nesting. Someone with ADD is not going to take the time to lift and nest so that she can puzzle each piece into its unique spot in the complex organizing system you've developed for your dish cabinet. She is just going to shove things—precariously—on top (as you have learned). Reducing the number of dishes in your cabinets to a reasonable number and retaining only those dishes that are of similar size so that they can be stacked—not nested in a graded tower—will make it much easier to manage the dishes.

De-Clutter Your Dish Cabinet

1 Remove anything from this cabinet that does not qualify as an everyday dish; you should be left with a stack of plates, salad plates, bowls, and, if the cabinet is large enough, glasses and mugs.

2 Discard any dishes that do not stack comfortably. It is acceptable to hold on to a series of bowls that are the same size but different colors, but you want to dispose of bowls that vary in size, because they might tempt you to nest smaller stacks inside and on top of larger stacks. You never want to have to lift one dish to get to another.

3 Reduce your stacking dish collection to a number that will comfortably fit in the space; this means that there must be empty shelf space between stacks, even when every dish in the house is washed and put away. (To achieve this, it might be necessary to get rid of your saucers entirely.)

4 When returning the stacks of dishes to the shelf, line them up next to each other, not in front or behind, so that nothing needs be shuffled around to retrieve or replace a dish.

5 Separate the glasses from the mugs and return them to their own separate shelves or areas. Do not keep more glasses and mugs than will comfortably fit on this shelf. Do not stack mugs—your goal for this whole cabinet is easy in/easy out.

Remember to make putting the dishes away as simple and easy as possible by designating the cabinet that is within **easiest reach** of the sink/dishwasher as the dish cabinet.

Dishwashing Diatribes

PROBLEM

"I tend to leave my clean dishes sitting in the dishwasher."

SOLUTION

If you're like others with ADD, you may be motivated to take a dish from the cabinet when you are hungry, but find little motivation to put the clean dishes away. By locating dish cabinets conveniently near the sink and dishwasher (cookware has the next priority for sink/dishwasher proximity), you increase the likelihood that you will put those clean dishes away.

"My sink is always overrun with dirty dishes."

A large number of crusty old, dirty dishes can be tedious and overwhelming for someone with ADD. To cut down on the unwashed mess, you first have to limit the number of dishes in your home. Keep only enough dishes to fill the dishwasher. It is better to be forced to run the dishwasher, or wash a small number of dishes more frequently, than to be continually confronted with large, unwieldy stacks of dirty dishes whenever you fall behind with your chores.

Use your china dishes only when absolutely necessary; it is quicker and more efficient to use paper plates as your "china" of choice at everything but your most formal meals.

Avoid moving food and dishes out of the kitchen. If you must have entertainment while you cook or eat, put a TV or radio in the kitchen. It is easier to find a corner for a small TV than to be constantly picking up dirty dishes and crumbs all over the house.

A dishpan with a jumbled, unfolded heap of towels, dishcloths, and sponges provides sufficient organization. Dishwashing liquid sits next to the sink and old and extraneous kitchen cleaning supplies have been eliminated so that the cabinet contains only those supplies for which there is an imminent need.

Dishtowel Dos and Don'ts

- *Clean sponges, dishtowels, and dishcloths* can be kept, jumbled and unfolded, under the sink in a plastic dishpan. There is no need to fold your clean dishtowels; as long as they are in a roomy, segregated and dry space, they are organized enough.

- Although hooks are nice, *dishtowels that are in active use* can just be thrown over the dish drying rack. Procure one if you don't already own one—every house needs a drying rack next to the sink as a visual cue to cleanliness; dishes left on the counter can too easily get mixed in with dirty dishes.

- *When your dishtowel is dirty,* throw it in the direction of the laundry room, perhaps dropping it at the bottom or top of a staircase if the laundry room is on another floor. If it's wet, you may need to slip it in a plastic bag first, so that it doesn't damage floors and carpets while it tarries in this staging area, waiting for you to scoop it up on your next voyage to that end of the house.

Solving the Dishwashing Dilemma

- Use attractive lidded enameled cookware that can double as serving and storage pieces.

- Substitute Tupperware for food prep and serving bowls.

- Locate the dish/cookware cabinets near the sink.

- Own only enough dishes to fill the dishwasher, so that you are motivated to run it regularly.

- Whenever possible, use paper plates and plastic.

- Whenever possible while baking or roasting, line your pan with tinfoil to ease clean up.

- Keep your kitchen garbage can open, convenient, and accessible—rather than tucked in behind a cabinet door under the sink—in order to simplify kitchen cleanup.

The Problem with Paper Products

PROBLEM

Open packaging, left over party supplies, an unnecessary variety of plate sizes, and a pickle jar with an inadequately small "mouth" for utensil storage, creates a stressful and inefficient paper storage space.

Reduce your paper stock to those items you regularly use; if you rarely use plastic wine glasses or disposable cups, then throw them out.

SOLUTION

Open packaging has been removed, leftover party supplies are almost used up—rather than saved for the next event—and utensils have been dumped into an open loaf pan. Smaller plates and novelty items were discarded to make more room.

Since you should be using paper plates for most of your meals, it is worth taking a couple of steps to ensure that these items are stored in an organized fashion. Designate a cabinet or shelf as the Paper Products Area, and then remove anything that is not a paper product from that space. Although it is acceptable to put an unopened stack of paper plates under the stack that you are currently using, it is imperative that the first time you take a plate from the new package, you discard the packaging. I cannot tell how often I transform a paper products area from unsightly and unusable clutter to an efficient and organized space, merely by removing all that plastic wrap that keeps everything from stacking nicely and interferes with everyone's ability to retrieve needed items.

Don't clutter your cabinets with a pack of turkey napkins and a half-dozen birthday cups that you are saving for next year; use up your decorative specialty napkins, cups, and plates in the days following your event.

Paper Simplifying Tools

- Keep a sizable basket—one that will hold a four- or five-inch stack of napkins—on your table. (Do not use a wire-rack-style napkin holder that stores the napkins upright; they never hold enough napkins and are awkward to load.)

- Procure a paper towel dispenser with a freestanding arm that allows you to drop your paper towels onto it in one simple motion. Those that force you to unscrew a decorative knob or play with a spring are inefficient.

- A loaf pan is a convenient tool for storing plastic utensils—just dump them in willy-nilly from the box. If you prefer a more organized look, use a drawer insert tray to divide your utensils.

Kitchen Garbage Gripes

PROBLEM

"My husband has ADD and never throws anything out. Even if it is obviously garbage—used napkins, banana peels, wrappers—he just leaves it on the kitchen counters!"

SOLUTION

Make your kitchen trash can more accessible. The number of steps it takes to access the trash can discourages your husband, so instead he leaves those gremlin-like gifts of garbage on the counters. Remove your trash bin from under the sink or counter, take off the lid, and place it in a convenient location. Or leave it under the counter, but remove the cabinet door. You want to make it as easy as possible for him to wing that refuse into the garbage.

"Our porch is always full of garbage bags that my ADD husband forgets to (or doesn't have time to) bring out on garbage day."

Moving the garbage to an out-of-the-way porch location is an inefficient extra step to taking out the trash and it drops the garbage off your husband's radar so he forgets to take it out. Further, the system of taking out all the garbage in one big chore on garbage day is very ADD-unfriendly, as it turns a series of small tasks into one big, overwhelming task. To solve this problem, make the stair landing your garbage staging area. Once a garbage bag fills, it should be left in front of the stairs (or the outside door) so that it is convenient for you or your husband, every time you leave your home, to scoop up the one or two bags that are blocking this primary exit and take them to the outdoor cans.

Trash Tips

- Make sure your kitchen garbage can is large enough. It is inefficient to be forced to empty it more than once daily.

- Store garbage bags conveniently, either next to the can, or at the bottom of the can underneath the current garbage bag. The contents of an entire box of garbage bags can live here without seriously affecting the volume of trash your bin can store.

Garbage Day Tips

- Place your garbage in a location that is directly in the path of your most-oft used exit from your home. When you leave the house, you will be forced to sweep it up and take it with you just to get out the door.

- Store your outdoor cans directly outside the door you most frequently use to exit your home; this will make it easy to dispose of the garbage as you go out.

Leave your outdoor garbage cans just outside the front door, so you can easily dump household trash as soon as you leave your house. As garbage bags may go to the outside can any day, but the can goes to the curbside only once a week, it makes more sense to keep the cans closer to your home than to the curb.

A Recipe for Recipes and Cookbooks

PROBLEM

"My recipes are a jumbled mess of magazine clippings, index cards, and notepaper shoved into cookbooks, but I don't have the time or focus to transfer them **all** to recipe box cards."

SOLUTION

Do not bother transferring recipes. Whether your recipe is torn from a magazine or scrawled on notebook paper, it will be easier to file away if you don't have to rewrite it on a standardized page. Striving for a uniform system adds steps. Plus, if all the index cards look alike, it will be harder to find the recipe you're looking for. Instead, put all of your recipes (those on cards, and those yet to be transferred) in a flex file folder with no more than eight sections. Label these sections by printing with a marker—no time-consuming label devices—the following categories: appetizers/soups/sauces, desserts, fish/seafood, meat/poultry, omelets/casseroles, salads/salad dressings, vegetables, miscellaneous. Your flex folder should be the size of a standard book so that it can be stored standing up with the other cookbooks. The flex-style folder system is superior because it is *not* uniform—you will, for example, easily retrieve Grandma's chicken soup recipe from the soup section because you will remember that it is the only recipe in that section written on the back of a greeting card.

> If you use a lot of cookbooks, then a small bookshelf will be a necessity in your kitchen.

Recipes, torn from newspapers and scrawled on the backs of greeting cards, are simply dropped into sections labeled with broad categories like "meat/poultry" and "desserts." The lack of uniformity makes the recipes easy to find.

Cleaning Supply Chaos

PROBLEM

"I keep most of my cleaning supplies in the kitchen, but I leave them all over the house."

Organization is about finding a balance between having enough duplicates to store things where you use them but not filling your storage areas with inventory or keeping too much "just in case" inventory in remote locations.

SOLUTION

Your cleaning supplies are scattered because you use them in other areas of your home. Remember the rule: Duplicate where necessary to store things where you use them. Storing things like cleaning supplies where you use them is particularly important in an ADD household, where jobs are easily started but not so easily finished. It is fine to stick with the traditional method of storing cleaning supplies under the kitchen sink or, if you have children, in a high kitchen cabinet. But you should have a duplicate set of cleaning supplies under every sink in the house. That way, cleaning supplies are quick and easy to retrieve the minute you notice a problem, and you can put them away with minimum fuss.

Also keep modest cleaning supplies handy for small spontaneous jobs. A container of disinfecting wipes or baby wipes along with a wastebasket should be stored in just about every room in your home. While it is doubtful that you will make the effort to fetch and then put away a bucket and damp rag for wiping down a smudged bureau top in the guest room, you might make a quick swipe if there is a wet wipe within easy reach, which you can then wing into a convenient wastebasket.

Check that you can see all of your cleaning supplies. If the shelves in your cabinet are too high, move supplies to a lower cabinet or hang a small spice-style shelf within reach on the inside of the cabinet door to corral smaller items.

Hiring a housekeeper for at least the bathrooms and floors is probably the most efficient and frugal expenditure of your resources when measured in currencies of time, stress, energy, and money.

CONTROLLING THE CLEANING CABINET

While it is best to duplicate cleaning supplies and store them where you use them, there will probably still be a large cluttered cleaning supply cabinet in the kitchen or utility room. Follow these five easy steps to get your supplies in order.

1 Call your town office and ask for the date of the next hazardous waste removal day, and then mark that day on your calendar with instructions to set aside twenty minutes to go through your cleaning supply cabinets.

2 On the chosen day, empty out the entire cabinet (or shelf) and set aside for disposal anything that has not been used in a year.

3 Clean out the bottom of the cabinet with paper towels.

4 Return only cleaning supplies to this cabinet, and of those, only products that you regularly use.

5 Drive your hazardous waste over to the collection site.

The Dining Room

Dining rooms tend to be one of the most underutilized spaces in a home. When they are messy, it is usually because adequate storage is not provided for formal dinnerware or because the top of the dining room table has become a dumping ground for backpacks and mail or it's the scene of an ongoing project. In fact, because many people with ADD are creative—artists, hobbyists, crafters—it often makes sense to either provide hobby supply storage in the dining room or re-designate it as a project room. If you retain this room for dining, then **all** dining room support items should find a home in the dining room, which means procuring dining room storage style furniture such as sideboards and breakfronts to house your formal china and table linens.

Is your dining room table cluttered with the materials of your latest unfinished project? For a smooth transition from project room to dining room, add a storage unit that allows you to quickly and easily clear out project supplies when it's time to dine.

The Messy Dining Room Table

PROBLEM

"My dining room table is often buried underneath craft projects and my son's school papers."

SOLUTION

Start by redefining your dining room as a dining room/project room. If you have semipermanent projects always laid out, then you will need to place a hobby storage unit in the dining room so that project support items can be *quickly and conveniently* swept out of sight before dining. If your son will be doing his homework on the dining room table, you'll need to provide a caddy for his stationery supplies, a recycling bin for completed homework, and a basket for blank notebook paper, and set them on one end of the dining room table. Leave an empty shelf in your dining room sideboard, so that when company comes, your son's "desk" (caddy and basket) can be quickly and handily swept out of sight. The recycling bin can be "toed" into the hall closet around the corner. Redefining this room, and your expectations for how this room will look, while employing appropriate storage to ensure that it can be transformed back into a formal dining room in under two minutes, will reduce your stress and allow you to use this room guilt free.

Tackle a messy dining room by adding extra light. Good lighting is an important organizational tool; rooms that are underlit become cluttered more readily, as it is just too much strain on the eyes to stow, retrieve, and organize items housed in dark cupboards and shadowy recesses.

A Jumble of Table Linens

PROBLEM

"I have trouble storing all my tablecloths and finding the right size when I need it. Should I photograph and measure my table-cloths and make a master list on the computer by color, size, and season?"

SOLUTION

Do not create an unnecessarily complicated and hard-to-maintain indexing system by photographing or applying a tape measure to your table linens. Instead, sort them into the sideboard, simply, by *table size,* not color, season, or inches. For example, a drawer might have two stacks of tablecloths—one stack fits the table when it has no leaves in it, the other fits the table when it has one leaf in it. Before a dinner party, it is more efficient to peruse all of your correctly sized options in a single glance than to be opening and rummaging through multiple drawers.

If your linens are always wrin-kled, you're probably stuffing too many into the drawers. While you are sorting your tablecloths by size, get rid of old, stained, and wrongly sized table linens to make room for the four or five that you use most often.

China Storage

When placing your dishes in your china cabinet, avoid using quilted holders. These holders never quite fit your inventory and require too many steps in order to put china away. Invariably, you will end up stacking dishes on top of the quilted holder. And while you may need them to guard against grime if you are storing dishes in the basement, in a dining room cupboard where dust is at a minimum, it is just simpler to stack the dishes directly onto the shelf. Even if the top plate gets dusty, it is easier to rinse it off than wrestle a heavy stack of brittle dishes into a limp, awkward cover.

If you serve formal meals, do not be misled into thinking that a china cabinet or breakfront is an extravagance. Innumerable homeowners pay me exorbitant sums to unclutter their kitchens, when all they really need is a china cabinet in their dining room. Your formal dishes and large serving pieces do *not* belong in the kitchen (nor certainly the basement)—it is an inefficient use of space that is probably causing the daily irritation of overcrowded kitchen cabinets.

> Anything that doesn't fit in your sideboard or china cabinets should be donated or consigned. Give it to a young relative starting up a home. Don't keep it for twenty years in the hopes that one day your kids will appreciate it.

A Case of Misplaced Dishes

A recent client with ADD proudly pointed to a series of basement shelves where her formal china and serving pieces were stored in quilted covers in organized splendor. When questioned, she admitted that although she had no trouble fetching these dishes for holiday dinners, they then languished on the kitchen counter for weeks before they were put away. This was a perfect example of beauty duping efficiency—talk about too many steps and inconvenience! I suggested putting a china cabinet in the dining room for these dishes. Not only would this make setting the table easier, it would keep her from stalling on putting the china away, since the dining room was right off the kitchen! And as an added benefit, moving the china opened up a lot of valuable basement shelf space, providing a home for all the basement-appropriate items lying cluttered on the floor.

Tips for Formal Dishware

- Store your formal china, serving pieces, and anything else that is used in the dining room in the dining room (keep everyday dishes and kitchen appliances in the kitchen). Do not store them in the basement where they will be forgotten.

- If you own more dishes and linens than will comfortably fit in your current dining room storage pieces, then you must procure more furniture or reduce your inventory.

- Although one or two decorative items, a soup tureen, or silver service may live on top of the sideboard, your goal is to keep it relatively clear of knick-knacks, so that it is always ready to serve its primary function as a staging area for serving dishes that don't fit on the table during formal meals.

Quilted holders, like the one in this image, should not be used as they inhibit efficient storage. It is easier to put a dish on a shelf than to wrestle it into a soft container.

CHAPTER 3

Adult Bedrooms

For someone with ADD, the bedroom can serve as both a refuge and a hub. All the many mediums—TV, stereo, laptop computer—and hobbies that the ADD client needs to engage his shifting attentions wander into the bedroom. The bed and floor are usually piled with magazines, CDs, dirty laundry, unfolded clean laundry, and packaging so that the client is often forced to enter the bed from the foot. Drawers hang open with excess clothing, and dresser tops are piled high with clothes that never made it into the drawers. Reducing the inventory that traditionally belongs in the bedroom down to a spare and manageable number and creating organizational systems for this inventory that the ADD client can manage are the first steps to providing a true bedroom refuge.

The Bedroom Floor

PROBLEM

"My bedroom floor is a mess, and I can't seem to keep up with it. It's covered in dirty clothes, tissues, shopping bags, and boxes."

SOLUTION

For starters, move any small wastebaskets to a convenient spot next to the bed for use as a tissue receptacle, and place a large kitchen-sized basket next to the bureau for packaging and old cosmetics. Sure, it's not pretty, but it's effective. Bringing down all of these trash items one by one to a central wastebasket in the kitchen or elsewhere in the house is too many steps for someone with ADD. It is more efficient to occasionally bring down a lot of trash in one garbage bag.

Every bedroom also needs an easily accessible hamper, meaning it should not be shut in your bedroom closet, as that adds a step to putting away dirty clothes. Look around your room—where does the largest pile of dirty laundry sit? The hamper goes as near as possible to the spot where you prefer to disrobe. Hampers should be large enough so clothes don't overflow before laundry day, but not so large that they are difficult to transport. A large plastic laundry basket is your best option for a hamper, since it is both easily transportable and naturally lidless. You want the hamper to be lidless so laundry can be tossed into it from almost any spot in the room. If you can just as easily toss a dirty sock into your hamper as onto your bedroom floor, you're on your way to a de-cluttered room.

Bed Making

PROBLEM

"My ADD husband **never** makes the bed. Even when I ask him as a special favor, he doesn't get it right."

SOLUTION

Simplify bed making so that your husband isn't sabotaged by too many steps while performing—out of love for you—a task he probably doesn't give a fig about to begin with. Designer beds with tons of pillows and shams are lovely to look at, but they require too much upkeep for someone with ADD, as they value beauty above efficiency. It is unlikely that your ADD husband will ever have the motivation to re-create this complicated "bed-scape." So get rid of any pillows but those on which you sleep. Also avoid multiple blankets and spreads. A puffy, thick comforter, quickly pulled up, will hide a plethora of bed-making errors. Spend your money on a gorgeous comforter, not on useless decorative pillows that are likely to languish on your floor.

Further simplify your bed making by positioning your bed away from the walls; there should be no impediment to walking around the bed while you are making it. Avoid lofts (and with kids, bunk beds), as they make it too awkward to change the linens.

Making Bed-Making Easy

- Place your bed away from the walls, so you have easy access to all sides.

- Keep only those pillows on your bed that you use to sleep—no decorative pillows and shams.

- Procure a single puffy comforter rather than scores of blankets and spreads.

- Remember that efficiency should always take preference over beauty.

Bed Linens

PROBLEM

"My bed linen closet is a mess, and I can't ever seem to find what I want."

SOLUTION

Eliminate the need for a bed linen closet altogether by reducing your linen inventory and then storing the remaining sheets in the room where they will be used. If there are multiple beds of the same size in the home, then you will need only one set of spare sheets in that size. Linens should come off the bed only when you are on the point of washing them, and then ideally that same set should return to the bed that same day. The extra set is for rare occasions.

Do not store your linens together in a central location. It is more efficient to store them near the bed for which they are intended. Reducing your linen inventory to two sets or fewer for each bed should make it easy to fit the linens on the closet shelf of their respective bedrooms. Finally, assign each bed a color to clear up any confusion about which sheets fit which bed.

Don't put sheets with your regular clothes laundry. They'll get wait-listed in the laundry line until you end up pulling out the spare sheets instead of cleaning them. Give each bed its own laundry day to increase the chances that the sheets will make it back onto the bed.

Bedside Mess

PROBLEM

"I like to do a lot of things in bed—read, work on my laptop, do a crossword puzzle—so there is always a big pile of junk on the floor next to my bed."

SOLUTION

Get a bedside table that will support all of the activities that you pursue in bed, and if you share a bed, make sure that you have a bedside table for each occupant. Each nightstand should be stocked with tissues and a lamp. If your large bedroom trash basket isn't convenient to the bed, then tuck a small wastepaper basket—handy for used tissues, completed crosswords, etc.—by the nightstand.

People with ADD tend to pursue a wider variety of activities in their beds than most people, so an adequate bedside table—large with shelving below—to support those activities is a necessity. Depending on the number and range of your activities, you may even wish to add a second bedside table next to the first.

Nightstand Know-How

Every person's needs and preferences will be slightly different, but two overriding principles are the same for all.

1 A nightstand is a necessity and must be large enough to support any activity that is pursued in bed.

2 Only that which you use in bed belongs on the nightstand.

Determine Your Nightstand Needs

The only items that belong on the bedside table are those items you use while lying in bed—a book, your glasses, some lotion, etc. Here is a simple chart to help you determine your storage needs:

IF YOU...	YOUR NIGHTSTAND NEEDS
Talk on the phone in bed	A paper and pen
Watch TV in bed	A space for the remote and the *TV Guide*
Use your laptop in bed	An open shelf to hold the laptop when not in use
Floss your teeth or blow your nose in bed	A small trash bin nearby
Take pills in bed	A drawer, a covered basket, or an easy-to-open box for private pill storage

The Buried Bureau

PROBLEM

"My bureau top is always buried under a pile of clothes and accessories because there's no room for it in my drawers."

SOLUTION

You will never put things away if your bureau is always bursting with clothes and you have to wrestle with it to open or close a drawer. Reduce your clothing inventory to an amount that will comfortably fit in your bureau drawers. Name your drawers and then store only those clothes that adhere to this name within that drawer.

Deal with your accessories next: Get rid of the old and dated, then divide your accessories into categories and assign each category a drawer. Go ahead and have a scarf drawer, but keep *only* scarves in it—do not make it a dumping ground for unrelated items. Larger drawers can be subdivided with a clear plastic box (shoe box size), creating a belt "drawer" and scarf "drawer." As long as the belts and scarves aren't mixed together, the drawer will be organized. If you still can't fit all of the clothes and accessories that you wear regularly into one bureau, purchase another one. While men can usually get by with one bureau, most women could probably use two or more to hold all their bras, hose, purses, scarves, shawls, slips, jewelry, and camisoles.

Keep your goals realistic: Once you have segregated all clothing items to their correct drawers and the drawers are not overflowing, your job is done. Don't aim for beauty by folding your underclothes or rolling up your socks into pairs; that's just a waste of your time and focus.

If an item of clothing is not yet ready for the laundry, then put it back in the drawer; do not worry that the lightly soiled clothing will "infect" the clean clothes, instead worry that piles of lightly worn clothes will infect your bedroom with clutter.

Remove from your bureau drawers anything that does not traditionally get used in a bedroom—packs of photos, papers, memorabilia, tools. Bureaus should be reserved for clothing, and clothing-type accessories **only.**

The Bureau Breakdown

- Women need at least two bureaus.

- Each bureau drawer should hold one category of clothing; if you must combine categories, then place clear plastic boxes in your drawers to divide them.

- Don't bother folding undergarments.

- Don't own more clothes than will fit into your bureau drawers; if the drawer won't close comfortably on laundry day, then you must purge items from your wardrobe.

The Sock Drawer Solution

PROBLEM

Socks of varying styles and colors, along with photos, stationery, a small jewelry box, a decorative plate and a complicated system of novelty pantyhose in plastic bags make this sock drawer a stressful and inefficient mess.

"I have a lot of unmatched socks in my drawer. I can't throw them out because every now and then I find the mate."

SOLUTION

Socks have been limited to one style in the two most frequently used colors, eliminating any need to match and roll. Panty hose and knee-highs have been reduced to the two most often used colors which were then segregated into separate clear plastic bins to prevent snagging.

Stop torturing yourself with this tedious sock-matching sadism. Throw these socks out, and when you find a mate, throw it out too. You will be down the cost of a couple of socks, but you will have gained time, drawer space, and peace of mind. In fact, throw out all of your socks. Identify a style of medium-weight sock that you can wear daily and buy a couple dozen of that style in two colors (for example, white and black). Voila! No more tedious matching issues—if you see another black sock in your drawer, you know you have a pair!

Hosiery Hindrances

PROBLEM

"My hose are always in a big jumble, and then I sometimes have to try on several pairs to find one that doesn't have a run in the wrong place."

SOLUTION

The joy of having ADD is that it's okay to be a little messy, as long as you can find what you need. Embrace the jumble—hose are organized enough if they have their own drawer or container within a drawer. A plastic bin or dishpan should keep pantyhose from snagging on old wooden bureaus. You may want to keep your hosiery in separate boxes to divide them by style (pantyhose versus knee-highs). As always, keep your inventory down to a number that fits comfortably in your storage area. This means you must throw out any pantyhose that are snagged; do not attempt a complicated system of "okay to wear with long skirts" or "okay to wear with boots."

Sock Drawer Wisdom

- Avoid storing miscellaneous items (passports, keepsakes, tissues) in your sock drawer.

- If your drawer is too big for your sock inventory, add another category (such as bras or pantyhose) to the drawer in a clear plastic box.

- Avoid the small diamond-shaped dividers that hold one sock only per bin. They will never conform to your number of socks, and they are too tedious to load.

> Throw out any pantyhose that are snagged; do not attempt a complicated system of "okay to wear with long skirts" or "okay to wear with boots."

The Jewelry Jinx

PROBLEM

"I'm constantly losing expensive jewelry—it really drives me nuts!"

The best place to store the bulk of your jewelry—even the most treasured items— is a clear, plastic, open tray, with built-in bins positioned in front of the mirror where you don it.

SOLUTION

Re-examine where you keep your jewelry. Storing it in a closed jewelry box or in a bureau drawer requires too many steps to put each piece away, so it will get dumped on the dresser top, only to be inadvertently knocked off and vacuumed up. If at all possible, avoid jewelry boxes, especially the ones that are just a series of little drawers—you are never going to remember which drawer holds what. The only kind of jewelry box I would recommend for someone with ADD is the old-fashioned, tiered kind that exposes all of the contents at once. Also, get rid of any small decorative boxes used for jewelry; it is inefficient to be opening and shutting a series of boxes and drawers in order to locate a particular piece.

The best place to store the bulk of your jewelry—even the most treasured items—is a clear, plastic, open tray, with built-in bins positioned in front of the mirror where you don it (even if that mirror is in the bathroom). This way, you can drop pieces into the appropriate tray bin with little effort, and you can see all of your jewelry at once. If you like, keep the jeweler's boxes for your most expensive pieces, but the jewelry itself should be kept in the tray. Necklaces that are large enough to slip over your head can be hung on pegs or hooks; adhesive-backed plastic hooks are easily installed by pressing them onto the wall in your jewelry area.

Procure enough trays so that every necklace and bracelet that can tangle (chain styles) has its own bin, with empty bins left over. Rigid necklaces and bangles can be stored together in one large tray. Earrings also go in trays with bins, but no bin should hold more than three pairs of earrings. Loosely organize your earrings tray by mentally naming the bins for color or style (pink, purple, blue, hoop, pearl, amber).

Jewelry is stored in open trays in front of the mirror where it is donned. Press-on plastic adhesive hooks hold longer necklaces. Note the advantage of improved visibility when comparing the clear tray to the milky tray.

Jewelry Storage Tips

- Jewelry should be stored in front of the mirror where you put it on.

- Long necklaces belong on hooks.

- Tiered trays and plastic trays of clear open bins are more convenient than multiple little drawers and covered boxes.

- Keep your jewelry boxes open and remove the lids from any jewelry trays.

- Small, tangle-prone necklaces and bracelets get individual bins in a clear jewelry tray. Rigid styles can go all together in a larger tray.

- Rings and pairs of earrings can go three to a bin in a jewelry tray.

- Maintain open bins.

- Get rid of all the packaging; do not keep little cardboard boxes and felt sleeves.

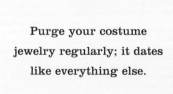

Purge your costume jewelry regularly; it dates like everything else.

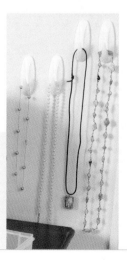

Press-on plastic adhesive hooks are perfect for holding longer necklaces

The Unmanageable Bedroom Closet

PROBLEM

"I paid for an expensive custom closet, but it's still disorganized!"

SOLUTION

Your closet is still disorganized because you built a complicated storage system instead of reducing your inventory. A custom closet is not an organizational necessity. All you really need for an organized closet are hooks, cheap stacking bins and shelves, improved lighting, the ability to purge, and a few clever organizational tricks.

Be realistic about the likelihood of wearing those too-small clothes again. Besides, by the time you do end up fitting back into that size six outfit, it will be hopelessly outdated.

Sliding closet doors should always be removed; they prevent you from seeing the entire closet at once.

Steps to Creating an ADD-Friendly Closet

1 Remove anything in your closet that is not wardrobe related, with the exception of one set of bed linens, and anything that is not yours. That's right, do not allow other family members to share your closet space.

2 Next, remove outdated, torn, ill-fitting, and novelty clothing until the size of your wardrobe comfortably fits in your closet space.

3 Improve the lighting in your closet or remove the door(s). If you can't see in your closet, you won't keep it organized. Sliding closet doors should always be removed; they prevent you from seeing the entire closet at once.

4 Install hooks in and around your closet for bathrobes, cardigans, and wet towels. You are more likely to use hooks than hangers.

5 Arrange your hanging clothes by length, so that you can utilize the space under your shorter clothes for extra storage.

6 Add cheap storage in the closet space you've created. Depending on your inventory (athletic clothing, shoes, hats, purses), some options include a shelf-style shoe rack, a stack of open-front bins, a cabinet of plastic drawers, or some cheap shelves. Assign only one category per bin or drawer.

You have now created your own custom closet for less than a hundred dollars! But keep in mind that no matter how much work you put into this, you will never get your closet organized if you aren't willing to toss out excess clothing and anything you haven't worn in a year. Purge with abandon!

Stacking bins hold accessories or corral supplies for activities –the top bin holds everything needed for a trip to the beach or pool.

Organizing by length creates storage space underneath hanging clothes. A shelf style rack is easiest for shoe storage and hooks provide easy storage for sweaters and robes. The top shelf holds an open bin for out of season clothes, a single change of linens, and a suitcase. Plastic hangers don't tangle and help to prevent over-crowding.

Arrange your hanging clothes by length, so that you can utilize the space under your shorter clothes for extra storage.

Do not allow other family members to share your closet space.

Clothes-Purging Tips

- Discard old, stained, shabby, and ill-fitting clothing; if you haven't worn it in a year, get rid of it.

- Do not own more clothing than you can comfortably fit in your closet.

- Make a list of your needs before shopping for clothes—avoid impulse purchases!

Clothes Hanging Hang-ups

PROBLEM

"I lay my clean clothing over a chair in my bedroom. My room-mate gets angry with me because I'm not hanging everything up in the closet."

Buy a dozen extra plastic hangers in one color. While you are switching your clothes from metal to plastic hangers, remove any foam from metal dry-cleaner hangers and slip it over the colored plastic hangers instead. Now you have easily identifiable hangers that are perfect for slippery silk or boatneck collars.

SOLUTION

We all avoid hanging up clothing if it requires waging war with a combative tangle of metal hangers, but those with ADD will not just delay battle, they will choose not to fight. The result is a layer of clothing covering the bedroom furniture and floors. Replace all those contentious metal hangers with some thick plastic hangers, as they do not readily tangle and help guard against overcrowding. Be sure to purchase plastic hangers with little hooks; they are invaluable for hanging up tops with spaghetti straps.

Hanger-Savvy Tips

- When clothes return from the dry cleaner, throw out the metal hangers the first time you remove the clothing to wear it.

- Throw out tiered hangers as well; they look space efficient, but they are too difficult to use. With the exception of suits, you are better off sticking to one item per hanger.

- Get rid of hangers that have swiveling necks. There is little advantage to using them, and they tend to wander into their neighbor's space.

- Large wooden hangers are acceptable so long as their necks don't swivel. They're nice for holding slacks and suits.

- Women should have a stash of skirt hangers; the "jaw" style is easiest to use.

Mounting Sportwear Solution

PROBLEM

"I am active in several sports, but I can't find a good way to organize all of my stuff. My tennis outfit, riding clothes, and the rest of it are just in a big pile on my bedroom floor."

SOLUTION

Keep the easy, one-step pile system, but modify it so that your piles of gear are up off the carpet and defined, rather than strewn about the floor. Pile your clothing in easy-to-access open-front plastic stacking bins (or for less frequently used items, plastic drawers) found at discount stores. Place these bins along your bedroom wall in place of the former piles, or tucked under short hanging clothing in the closet. Support items for sports or activities can be assigned to these bins. For example, you might need a workout bin, tennis gear bin, or beach support bin. Substitute the slightly less convenient plastic drawers for large categories like skiwear (which may include puffy pants and other outerwear).

Open-front bins are also useful for wardrobe accessories such as scarves, shawls, or belts. There is no need to fold or organize the contents. As long as each bin holds one category or activity only, you will have achieved an efficient and easy, though not particularly beautiful, organizational system for your wardrobe accessories, activities, and athletic endeavors.

Tie Tantrics

This layered tie rack hides all but the topmost ties, makes it hard to restore or retrieve ties, and is overwhelmed by the number of old and dated ties.

"I have tried many different styles of tie hangers for my ADD husband's ties, but no matter what I buy, he never returns the tie to the rack."

A towel bar provides easy access and good visibility after ties are pared down to the half dozen that are regularly used. Ties that were purchased to coordinate with a particular suit should be stored with that suit.

Reduce his tie collection to that half dozen or so he regularly wears or any that coordinate with his favorite shirt or suit. Once you have gotten rid of any old, stained, dated, or unworn ties, replace complicated tie racks with a simple towel bar or rod. Good tie racks display your ties, keep them easily accessible, and most important, do not require much effort when you put your ties away. Bad tie racks obscure most of your ties and require the close attention and fine motor skills of a Tantric guru when the time comes to return a tie to the rack. If your tie rack has pegs that are close together, is tiered, or swings, then it probably requires too much effort to be convenient. For better tie organization, install a simple towel bar or a horizontally mounted, arm-style paper towel holder on the closet wall or door so your husband can quickly and haphazardly drape his worn ties over it.

If you have a tie that is **only** and **always** worn with one suit, then store it with that suit; this will cut down the number of steps it takes to put your clothes away.

For better tie organization, install a simple towel bar or a horizontally mounted, arm-style paper towel holder on the closet wall or door.

Shoe Rack Blues

PROBLEM

"I bought wire shoe racks and a hanging shoe bag—the kind with a pocket for every pair of shoes, but they are now mostly empty and my shoes are all over the floor."

SOLUTION

Accept that your most frequently worn shoes should be kept on the closet floor. Pick one or two pairs that you wear most frequently and leave them there. Spindly wire racks and floppy shoe bags require too much effort; replace them with bookcase-style shoe racks. This simple shelf style requires the least amount of steps to store your shoes and is most versatile for different styles of shoes. Place the rest of your shoes—dress shoes, out-of-season shoes, and specialty shoes—on the shoe shelves. If you have no empty shelf space, purge your shoe collection down to only the number of shoes that will fit comfortably on the new rack.

Athletic shoes can be stored in stacking, open-front plastic bins (see "Mounting Sportwear Solution", on p. 89) with their commensurate clothing, so your child's tap shoes will be in a bin with her leotard and tights. If space is constrained, you may also wish to store out-of-season summer shoes in an open-front plastic bin or drawer (winter boots will be too big).

> Regularly purge old and unused shoes so your closet shoe shelf has plenty of room for shoes of all seasons.

Bookcase-style shoe racks require the least amount of effort to store your shoes and can accommodate various shoe styles.

ADD-Unfriendly Shoe Racks

Avoid the following types of shoe racks—they're less efficient than you think:

- Canted wire racks: Heel-less shoes fall off, and it requires too much effort to fit even the heeled shoes on the wire-bar-style racks.

- Cubby-style racks: It is too difficult to thread shoes into them, they cut down on visibility, and the cubbies are too small for boots or even men's larger shoes.

- Shoe boxes: They stack well, but it is too much work to put them away.

- Hanging shoe bags: It is just too much effort to stabilize a swinging shoe bag while you try to fit a shoe into a pocket or cubby.

- Benches that allow you to pull out a front panel "mailbox style": You can't pull out the front panel while sitting on the bench; instead, you will have to go through a multistep process of standing, turning, and bending.

The Seasonal Clothing Switch

PROBLEM

"How should I store my out-of-season clothes? I hate doing it, and I usually give up mid-job, and by the time I finally finish, it's time to switch them back."

If you must switch clothing out of your drawers, schedule this activity for the day after the laundry is done; you don't want to be continually plagued by stragglers that dillydallied in the wash.

SOLUTION

The quickest way to organize and simplify your seasonal clothing switch is to eliminate it altogether. Most bedrooms have enough wall space to accommodate a second (men) or even third (women!) bureau. You don't want to go through the laborious task of switching all of your clothes every season; it's just easier to address a different bureau. Designate the larger bureau as your winter bureau because winter clothing is thicker. Be sure to limit your wardrobe to only that which fits in each bureau—only summer clothes in the summer bureau, etc.

If you absolutely do not have room for a second bureau and so must switch clothes, make the seasonal switch easier by storing out-of-season clothes in a trunk at the foot of your bed or in a clear bin on the top shelf of your closet. Rely on your creativity to come up with a way to store out-of-season clothing in your bedroom in order to avoid the task of hauling awkward boxes to the attic or basement. And of course, do not retain more out-of-season clothing than you can comfortably store in your bedroom.

Many people use the seasonal switch to weed through their clothing. This may be suitable for most, but for someone with ADD, it can be overwhelming to do both tasks at once. Make the task more manageable by picking one overcrowded drawer and weeding out gifts, items that are shabby or ill fitting, and anything you haven't worn in a year.

Clothing of Sentimental Value

Sentimental clothing should be kept to a minimum, and consideration should only be given to those pieces that don't appropriate too much storage space. By all means, keep your grandmother's handkerchief, but let go of her tweed coat. Your son's first outfit (8 pounds, 20 inches!) and christening gown may be stored in a lovely baby memento box; his Little League uniform and the outfit he wore on the first day of kindergarten must go. Keep your wedding dress and prom dress, or your letterman's jacket and championship football jersey. Two items will not crowd your closet. If you promise not to take advantage, I'll even approve of storing them in the back of the guest room closet, but keep the purloining of others' closet space to a minimum. As for the rest of it, although people with ADD will hang on to "broken-in" comfy clothing longer than most, once they are done with a piece, they don't seem to struggle with the closure issues that can plague the rest of the population. So once you no longer wear an item regularly, tell yourself that you are not a vintage clothing store and when it comes back in style, you can get one that isn't fraying. Then send it all off to Goodwill.

Kid Bedrooms

As much as possible, you should arrange your children's bed-rooms—and lives—in a way that encourages reasonable and sustainable organizational habits. Giving your child the ability to control his or her own space and possessions fosters self-esteem. How do you accomplish this? For starters, provide enough storage space in the child's bedroom so that it is quick and easy for him to put things away. An ADD child is not going to put his toys away if he must shift and re-arrange his possessions to make room. To keep his bedroom clean, he needs a hamper, a garbage can, and some shelving. It's equally important to purge old and dated clothes and toys, so that the number of your child's possessions is not overwhelming to manage and there is plenty of empty storage space. By providing adequate storage and limiting possessions, you will have simplified the cleaning process so that it is within your child's capability to experience success.

Retain your child's room for his possessions only; do not allow other family members to use his closet or bureau.

Small Child, Big Mess

PROBLEM

"There is no way that my ADD preschooler is ever going to be able to clean his room."

SOLUTION

Although your expectations for perfect order will need to be adjusted if your child has ADD, there should still be some expectations for that child. Enable your child to clean his own room by providing easy storage solutions and keeping the number of his possessions down to a manageable level.

Reducing steps and materials is even more important for children than adults. If this means paring your ADD child's bedroom possessions down to two stuffed animals, a toy truck, and half a dozen books, then so be it. His self-reliance and consequent self-esteem is more important than all that plastic.

The most accessible form of toy storage you can provide for your child is a simple shelving unit. Place lidless tubs or open-front bins on the shelves where he can help store his collections of smaller toys. Avoid toy boxes or baskets of stuffed animals. They take up too much floor space without giving vertical storage, and your child will have to dump out the entire contents to get to an item on the bottom.

Now that you have all the right tools in place, give your child small chores that you know he can accomplish (picking up the stuffed animals instead of the whole room, for example), and stay with him during the chore to keep him on track. When he is done, cover him with praise—ADD children thrive on immediate gratification.

Tips to Help an ADD Child Organize

- Adjust your expectations for perfect order.

- Stay with your child through the room-cleaning process to lend him focus.

- Reduce the number of materials in his room so that it is simple and easy to clean.

- Make sure his storage systems are easy to access (low-hanging shelves and hooks).

- Limit the scope of his chore.

- Praise him lavishly when he completes it.

If your child's bedroom is also his playroom, then arrange the furniture so that the toy area is separate from the dressing area; it just makes the room easier to clean.

The Unmade Bed

If your child has ADD, you will have to pick your battles, and bed making is likely to be the first battle you will jettison. Nonetheless, on those occasions when it is important that the bed be made, you will want to simplify the chore in order to enable your child to manage it. Of course, this will not be a perfectly made bed, but it can be good enough for the child to feel a sense of accomplishment and independence.

- Avoid bunk beds and lofts—they're too difficult to make up.

- Pull your child's bed away from the wall, so that he can easily walk around it to pull up the bedding.

- Reduce the bedding to a sheet, a comforter, and one pillow, so that he need only pull up the plush (thick-enough-to-hide-rumpled-sheet-beneath) comforter, and plump the pillow to create a reasonably made bed.

- Rid the bed of all but one, or at most two, stuffed animals.

Even the most distractible child can occasionally manage to make up a bed if he need only pull up the comforter, plump his pillow, and place one stuffed animal near the headboard.

Bureaus: The Bigger the Better

Do not use a small bureau for your child's clothes. Although all of his clothing may comfortably fit into four small drawers now while he's wearing size four, soon enough you will need that extra space for size twelve. In the meantime, you can use the upper drawers of a larger bureau to keep more formal or special clothing out of your child's reach. Lower drawers should be reserved for those play clothes, socks, and underwear that he uses most frequently. Each drawer is then given a specific name, such as "sock drawer," "underwear drawer," "shirt drawer," or "pants drawer," so that he can, as much as possible, retrieve his own clothes and make sense out of how to put his own clothing away.

If your child impulsively pulls clothing from her drawers or changes her outfit several times a day, you may wish to reverse the order of the drawer contents to limit access to the clothing. Keep a couple of outfits in the lower drawers she can reach, but draft the higher, less accessible drawers, and the upper closet shelf, for the bulk of her wardrobe (just make sure that the bureau won't fall forward from being too top heavy). Household stress will be greatly reduced if Mom isn't picking up her toddler's entire wardrobe every time she enters the bedroom, and a two-year-old can clean up the mess he has made if it merely consists of returning half a dozen items to his drawers.

> Use bureau drawers for clothing only; do not mix in toys, books, and mementos, as this will forever sabotage the ADD child from keeping an organized room.

> Do not keep an extensive wardrobe for your ADD child—he will never be able to manage drawers that are overstuffed and overstocked. Constantly purge clothing that is old, too small, too stained, or that isn't worn because it doesn't "feel right."

Excessive Kid Clothing

PROBLEM

"My son has tons of clothes, but he won't wear most of them because the seams bother him or the material is too 'scratchy.'"

SOLUTION

Get rid of the clothes he won't wear and buy duplicates of those clothes he will wear, whenever possible. Many ADD children exhibit tactile hypersensitivity, but there are ways for you to make them more comfortable and get more value out of clothing purchases. For example, let your son wear his underclothing inside out if he wants. This really helps to reduce any irritation from seams. When purchasing socks for such a child, buy one pair in many different styles. Keep the socks with their packaging so that when you discover one that "feels right," you can go out and buy two-dozen pairs of that brand. Donate the "reject socks," and accept that although this method is expensive, it is the most efficient way to get through the morning dressing ritual. This method also works with underwear.

Do not give up on a new shirt or pants for your ADD child until you have run it through the wash several times and cut out the tags. He or she will be much more comfortable if multiple washings have softened the fabric and the clothes are either tag free or the tags have been removed. And for goodness' sake, don't bother sewing up the little hole that often results from tag removal. You have an ADD child; you have neither the time nor the energy to be repairing little tears that are probably hidden under her hair in any case.

The Dirty Laundry Dilemma

I was recently hired by an ADD mother to help her organize the shared bedroom of her eight-year-old twin boys and the room of her ten-year-old son. When I urged this mother to place an open laundry basket in the boys' rooms, she replied that she didn't mind (and it was just as easy) scooping the clothes off the floor on laundry day.

Unfortunately, leaving the dirty clothes all over the floor contributed to a distracting play area and generally messy room. After all, there is no point in picking up one's toys if there is always dirty clothing strewn about. This mother's efforts would have been better spent in procuring a couple of lidless hampers and placing them in a prominent spot in the boys' bedrooms.

Although it would have been difficult for her to change her routine, and it would have taken some energy to urge the boys to use the hampers, in the end, enabling them to care for themselves would have promoted an organized and appropriate play space, valuable social skills, and—someday—grateful daughters-in-law.

Do place a lidless hamper in a prominent location in your child's bedroom—no tucking it into a closet. I always recommend a tall laundry basket for this purpose; it makes for an easy target when tossing in dirty clothes.

Teenager Troubles

PROBLEM

Although the furniture is adequate, none of the shelves or surfaces have been named so this teen has no guide for organizing her possessions.

"My teenager has a large room with plenty of storage, but she is hopeless at keeping it organized."

SOLUTION

Naming the shelves—"books," "sentimental items," "athletic accessories"—immediately creates order. Beauty products have been corralled into open baskets to help clear off the dresser surface.

Do a quick purge of old or dated possessions. Next, identify your daughter's interests and activities and then designate convenient centers for each category. Provide storage for activity support items within those areas so that it is efficient (requires the fewest steps) for her to put things away. For example, in one teenage girl's room, a middle shelf from each of two shelving units that "bookended" her dresser were designated for use as ancillary "vanity table" storage. Using these shelves guarded her bureau top from burial under an extensive collection of beauty products. A couple more shelves within this shelving unit were then designated for books. One shelf was appointed the task of holding open-front bins for her dance and soccer clothes, and another for displaying decorative objects. The most inaccessible shelves at the top were used to display those toys for which she still had a sentimental attachment, but never needed to touch. I was careful to leave empty shelving space as a staging area for school projects, etc. By *defining* each shelf (vanity, books, display, athletics, staging, sentimental items), we gave this ADD teen a clear and easy map to cleaning her room, and by weeding her possessions, we ensured that she need never rummage or juggle to put things away. .

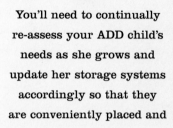

You'll need to continually re-assess your ADD child's needs as she grows and update her storage systems accordingly so that they are conveniently placed and easy to maintain..

Teenager Troubles

PROBLEM

"My teenage daughter's room is a disaster—every surface is covered with stuff—you can't even see the top of her dresser!"

SOLUTION

Teenagers require more shelving in their rooms than adults do. They just tend to hold on to more possessions and are often involved in a variety of activities that result in a buildup of stuff. First, have your daughter purge clothing, toys, and dresser-top decor that she's outgrown. If the top of your teenager's dresser is still overcrowded, buy a second dresser to act as a vanity and accommodate the growing supplies of a young woman, such as makeup, hair dryer, jewelry, and lotion. Purchasing one or two tall shelving units is another way to create versatile storage for your ADD daughter's changing needs.

For a teenage boy whose computer games or athletic equipment have taken over his bedroom, get rid of his old Lego table or child dresser and obtain some tall shelves for computer game storage and some open-front bins and hooks for athletic gear.

How to Organize the Bedroom of an ADD Teenager

1 Remove any games, toys, and clothes that are no longer developmentally appropriate.

2 Identify those activities that the teen *currently* pursues in the bedroom—listening to music, reading, playing computer games, etc.

3 Choose a single activity and designate an area for it—listening area, reading area, computer area, dressing area, etc.

4 Introduce furniture and storage that can support this activity and place it in the appropriate activity area.

5 Corral support items for this activity into the appropriate storage—*all* books on book shelf, *all* beauty items in vanity area.

6 Remove any intruders from the designated area—no clothes on the bookshelf, no makeup on the computer desk.

7 Get rid of excess; do not keep more "stuff" than can easily be stowed in the storage unit for that area.

8 Maintain through controlled shopping and constant purging; if the bookshelf fills up, get rid of some books before you buy more.

The Laundry

Laundry is the kind of chore that can bedevil those with ADD. Because it's an intermittent chore that requires lugging clothes all over the house, it encourages distraction while discouraging follow-through. Although there are a couple of organizational tricks of the trade that we can apply (such as duplication, sufficient laundry baskets, storing the ironing board where you use it, etc.) and a couple of specialized tools that can abate some of the challenges (an egg timer), we will only truly succeed in lightening the load by applying our two basic rules for efficiency: reducing the steps and reducing the materials.

Pile Avoidance

PROBLEM

"I start to fold the laundry, but then I get called away or see something else that needs to be done, so there are always piles of clean unfolded laundry on my couch, table—all over the house!"

SOLUTION

To prevent this scattering of clean clothes, choose *one* place in the house—a section of your laundry room, the dining room table, or better yet a bed in the guest room—as your laundry folding area so that clean laundry stays in one place. If you must fold laundry in front of a TV, then procure a small TV or radio for your chosen folding area. It is easier to set up a TV in this location than to deal with piles of laundry at various TV-viewing stations like the couch or kitchen table.

Never dump out your clean laundry! Keep your unfolded laundry in the basket, picking out one item at a time to fold. By placing only the folded laundry on the bed or table, and keeping the unfolded laundry in the basket, you will maintain an organized and stress-free laundry folding area. If you find that you are dumping because you need the laundry basket, then buy more baskets. Do make sure that all of your laundry baskets are the same shape so that they can nest comfortably when not in use.

Do make sure that all of
your laundry baskets are
the same shape so that
they can nest comfortably
when not in use.

Choose one area only
for laundry folding and
never dump out your
clean clothes.

Laundry Overload

One way to avoid becoming overwhelmed by laundry duty is to limit the size of your loads. Here are a few ways to keep laundry loads to a manageable minimum.

- Limit the number of clothes you own. Dresser drawers must not be over-stuffed, especially at the end of laundry day, or you will never bother to put your laundry away.

- Reduce your clothing inventory to just enough to get by; this will force you into doing frequent smaller loads rather than infrequent large, unwieldy loads—and the house won't be littered with enormous piles of clean laundry.

- Avoid purchasing clothing that has special laundry instructions; this type of clothing will get worn only once.

- Permanent press is your savior because it keeps clothes wrinkle free; avoid purchasing clothing that needs to be ironed.

The ADD-Appropriate Laundry Room

To create a more ADD-appropriate laundry room, you'll need to remove anything from the room that is not laundry-related. If the shelf above your washing machine is hosting extra blankets or household cleaners, this cluttered environment will sabotage your ability to efficiently attend to the laundry. Once you have cleared out items that don't belong, consider adding the following laundry organizational tools:

- **Trash bin:** Keep a kitchen-sized garbage can in the laundry room for lint, irredeemably shabby clothing, and general trash.

- **Donation bin:** A tall kitchen-sized wastebasket lined with a plastic bag should live in the laundry room, or wherever you fold laundry, so it is convenient for donations. Items you don't wear should come out of the laundry and go right into the donation bag. When the donation bin is full, tie off the plastic bag and throw it in the direction of the car, so it will be on hand next time you pass a clothing drop.

- **Egg timer:** Invest in an obnoxiously loud egg timer with no automatic shutoff. The buzzer on most washers and dryers switches off after a couple of seconds, but your egg timer should emit a loud, relentless beep until you actually go to the laundry room to shut it off. This will prevent laundry from loitering in the machine. And this type of timer will keep you on track and prevent laundry duties for dragging on too long.

- **Ironing board:** Store the ironing board and iron wherever it is that you like to iron. If you iron in front of the TV in the guest room, then ironing supplies belong in the guest room closet as opposed to

the laundry room. That said, make your life easier and don't buy clothes that require ironing.

- **Dishpan:** If you are lucky enough to have a sink in your laundry room, then you will want a plastic dishpan on hand for soaking stained garments (never leave soaking garments in the sink, since that obstructs you from using the sink). Otherwise, the dishpan and stain remover should live under the nearest sink, be it in the bathroom or kitchen, as that's where you will be filling and draining it.

- **Laundry baskets:** Make sure you own a sufficient number of laundry baskets, and that these laundry baskets are of a like shape so that they can compactly nest when not in use. A variety of colors will give you visual reminders of the type of laundry in that particular basket. Avoid the canvas bag on a wooden frame style hamper—it is not easily portable. Even the bedroom hampers should conform to an open portable basket style.

> Avoid the canvas bag on a wooden frame style hamper— they are not easily portable.

Making Laundry a Group Effort

Everyone over the age of six should contribute to doing the laundry. An ADD parent does the entire household a service when she empowers her non-ADD children to manage their own laundry. ADD children will need more supervision at an older age, but as long as their wardrobes are kept to a reasonable size, they too should be able to manage some portion of their laundry. Here are several family laundry plans. Choose the one that works best for your family:

- The "laundry day" system: Set out baskets the night before laundry day so that every family member can sort his or her own dirty clothes. You may have to put signs for "whites" and "colored clothes" on the wall above the baskets until every family member becomes familiar with the system. An adult then spends the day cycling the sorted wash through the machines. When the laundry is finished, family members become responsible for folding and/or putting away their own clothes. The whole family should fold and put away together—this will help to keep the ADD family member on track and prevent unclaimed clothes from piling up.

- The "daily laundry" system: Schedule one day of the week for each family member's laundry. The baskets are then left out permanently, and family members become responsible for sorting their dirty laundry the night before their scheduled washday and for folding and stashing their own clean laundry at the end of laundry day. An adult loads and unloads the washer and dryer for younger children.

- The "every man for himself" system: If you are the only ADD member of your family, and your children are ten or older, then household stress will be reduced if every family member is responsible for his or her own laundry.

> Every bedroom in your home should have a dirty laundry hamper. Use tall, portable laundry baskets with no lids so family members can simply "wing" their dirty clothes inside with minimal hassle.

CHAPTER 6

The Living Room/ Family Room

There is often one room of the home that serves more than one function as a family gathering area: It might be both a space to entertain guests and a children's play area. In an ADD home, the room might also serve as an art studio or craft area. Bills will be paid and meals consumed in front of the TV. Tools, art supplies, computer support paraphernalia, papers, and dishes will all migrate into the family room. With so many functions, it's no wonder that living rooms and family rooms are often the eye of the clutter storm. To curb this problem, you will first need to divide your common room into "zones" or areas. As long as you keep the activities and support items for your areas separate, you will avoid major clutter.

Family Room Fiasco

PROBLEM

"I use the living room for doing arts and crafts projects, watching television, surfing the Web on my laptop, and folding laundry. My husband gets angry that all my stuff is in the way."

SOLUTION

Many people with ADD are highly creative, and typically they divide their attention among several activities. If you pursue many of your activities in the family room, make a comfortable and reasonable place for those activities; then, in the interest of family harmony, reduce your inventory to an amount that will fit in that space and acquire storage to support it.

Your husband will prefer it if you leave the couch, coffee tables, and end tables open for family use and find additional space for your various activity supplies. How do you create this additional space? Place a long table with a rolling chair behind the living room couch and add a series of tall shelves within reach of the rolling chair. This way, you can paint, sew, craft, fold laundry, or use your laptop at the table and still see the TV without crowding the couch or the coffee table with stuff. Designate one bank of shelves of a nearby shelving system for tools/materials associated with each activity: painting materials, sewing tools, craft supplies, and computer accessories. An empty shelf shall be maintained on each shelving unit and should be designated as a staging area for projects in progress. A rolling tabletop cart—outfitted with a brake lock for stability—can provide a secondary working surface for you—in front of the TV—that can easily be moved aside or adjusted when traffic in your home increases at the end of the day. If any category of supply starts to grow out of its designated shelf space, you must donate or toss until it again fits on its appropriate shelves.

Top Three Living Room Organizational Tools

- A long table and rolling chair that can be placed behind the sofa
- Tall shelving units
- A rolling, tabletop cart

Creating a Family-Friendly Room

A mother of three young children, two of whom were hyperactive, found that her family seldom used the family room and that her kids often dragged their toys and mess into the kitchen to play. She hired me to help her create a better play area in the family room with ample toy storage to solve this problem. When I got there, I realized that the family room's main deterrent was not the toy clutter, but the furniture arrangement. In a loving attempt to accommodate her overly active children, this mother had pushed the comfy furniture back against the walls to create a large center play area. Although this arrangement was conducive for hyperactive gross motor play (and maybe the Embassy Ball), it was disastrous for family time. No conversation or close contact was possible with everyone facing the same direction or twelve feet apart. Further, this arrangement encouraged overstimulation and wildness, as even when seated, the kids had to raise their voices to communicate across the cavernous open room.

Instead of dividing this room into "center" and "edge," I placed the couch and chairs in a close conversational grouping with the TV on the far side of the room. By clustering the couch and chairs, we gained a small "behind the couch" alcove for supplementary toy storage shelving. And by putting the rest of the toys against the walls on the "play" side of the room, we were able to leave open a center area for that all-important gross motor play.

A rolling tabletop cart—outfitted with a brake lock for stability—can provide a secondary working surface for you—in front of the TV—that can easily be moved aside or adjusted when traffic in your home increases at the end of the day.

You may need to maintain open space in your family room, but make sure there is also a cozy conversation area for your family to gather and get comfortable. ADD children need cuddle time with you as much as they need space to spread out and play.

Food and the Family Room

To keep your family room in some type of order, make it a family rule that meals, snacks, and treats are *not allowed* in the family room. *Adults only* may have an occasional drink in there, but food should be confined to the kitchen. If you need entertainment while you eat, put a TV or radio in the kitchen. It is easier to add a small appliance to the kitchen than to be constantly scrubbing sticky jelly fingerprints from the walls, vacuuming crumbs from the couch, washing juice stains from the rugs, and gathering dirty dishes from every corner of the house. Free yourself from all that extra labor by sticking to the no food rule.

End tables make great living room staging areas. They do not accumulate clutter as one might think—instead they reduce clutter by keeping it off the floor.

Matching Activities with Storage Needs

Here are some typical activities done in the family room along with the tools that support them:

LIVING ROOM ACTIVITY	STORAGE NEEDS
TV viewing	Adjacent bookshelf for DVDs Open, shallow basket for remotes An ottoman for feet End table near favorite recliner for drink
Computer game playing	Open basket for remotes/rumble packs/joysticks Low table in front of TV Shelving for game storage
Reading	Good reading light Comfy reading chair End table for drink Shelves for books Rack for magazines

Obsolete Electronics

PROBLEM

"My ADD husband still has every computer he has ever owned. He even has his old stereo and turntable, although he only listens to music at the computer."

SOLUTION

Call your town office to find the date of your next hazardous waste day, mark it on your calendar, and then cut the cord. The multi-step process of electronic disposal can be overwhelming for someone with ADD, especially if he is under the impression that these items are valuable or should be donated. Assure him that these items are of little value due to obsolescence and that it is just too much effort for a family that includes ADD to micromanage used electronic equipment.

Don't hang on to an old CD walkman when you just got a new MP3 player. As soon as your electronics become redundant or outdated, donate them to charity.

Clearing Out Your Electronics

1 Dispose of redundant devices and old electronic equipment the minute you have a newer model. For example, get rid of your old television as soon as you purchase an HDTV.

2 For old and obsolete items, schedule a special pick-up with your waste removal company or call the town office to find out the next hazardous waste day.

3 Mark the day on your calendar and move the equipment out near the car or garbage area. Keep it visible, so that you have a constant reminder to complete this chore on garbage day/hazardous waste day.

4 Mark the date on a sticky note and stick it on the item as a second visual reminder of when you need to take it to the curb or to the hazardous waste collection site in your town.

Media Mayhem

PROBLEM

The awkwardness of manipulating CDs into this horizontal style CD rack is so discouraging that CDs rarely get put away.

"How can I keep all my CDs and DVDs organized? They are all over the family room!"

SOLUTION

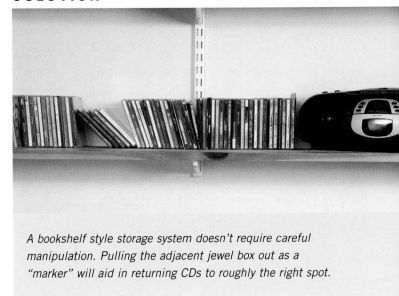

A bookshelf style storage system doesn't require careful manipulation. Pulling the adjacent jewel box out as a "marker" will aid in returning CDs to roughly the right spot.

Assign each electronic component—TV, stereo, and computer—separate areas and then place a unit of easy-to-access storage next to each component. Bookcase-style shelving is the easiest method for storing music and computer CDs and DVDs; avoid wire racks, which require an inordinate amount of fine motor skills and close attention to level each CD into an individual slot. Pare your CD collection down to a reasonable level (disks of obsolete computer programs should be the first to go) and place the ones you're going to keep on the shelves. Maintain realistic expectations: Accept that no matter what kind of storage you use, some members of your household will *never* put away a CD. However, if you have defined separate areas for your computer CDs, your music CDs, and your DVDs, it's more likely that items will stay in the general vicinity of their respective areas.

Overorganized CDs

PROBLEM

"I've arranged my CDs by category and printed out neat labels, but my ADD wife rarely puts anything back, and when she does, it's not in the right place."

SOLUTION

Instead of organizing by category, try using the simplest organizational method around: the alphabet. Your wife is probably discouraged by the challenges and effort involved in deciding whether Santana is rock or Latin, and whether Frank Sinatra sings Benny Goodman is big band or swing. Once you've simplified the system by making it alphabetical, suggest that when she takes a CD off the shelf, she pulls out an adjacent CD for a quick visual reference of where it belongs.

I discourage all of my clients from building up large collections of … well, anything, including DVDs and videos. How many times can one watch a movie? And isn't there a video rental store down the street that would be happy to manage this entire inventory for you? For ADD clients, for whom putting things away is so much more laborious, the structure of a "due date" can help to keep their inventory down and their family rooms picked up.

Tips for Media Management

- **Collections:** Don't collect. The most efficient system is the one that doesn't require managing inventory—think pay-per-view, MP3, and good old-fashioned radio.

- **Manuals and warranties:** User guides for TVs, CD players, etc., should be kept as near to the TV or CD player as possible—not in a binder in some remote room. If there is a drawer or cabinet near your TV, slip the manual inside it. If not, stash it behind the TV, leaving a corner visible so you won't forget it's back there. If you know how to operate the equipment, don't be afraid to throw out the manual.

- **Remotes:** A large, open, shallow basket conveniently located on your coffee table or end table is an easy target in which to drop the remote. Choose the table that can be reached—without stretching or bending—when you are sitting in your favorite chair.

- **The box it came in:** Throw out all of the space-gobbling packaging that came with your electronic components. Wait a week after setting up your new equipment—if it doesn't appear to be a lemon, then go ahead and throw out the box. If you move, you can always find another box.

The Playroom

An ADD parent, and the parent of an ADD child (who may manage to play with every single item in the playroom in one day), will greatly benefit from an efficient playroom organizational system. Your ultimate objective in organizing the playroom is to limit the amount of toys. One common mistake made by parents of ADD children is to provide extra toys because the children are so distractible. This is unnecessary, as an ADD child's creativity allows him to use a small number of toys in many novel and imaginative ways. Limiting the number of his toys will help to foster that creativity along with the self-reliance and self-esteem that come with picking up and putting away his own possessions without any help. Likewise, an ADD parent is not going to have the motivation or stamina to organize large collections of toys for his or her child. The less crowded your playroom becomes, the less stress and disorder you will be forced to endure.

Toy Migration

PROBLEM

"My ADD son picks things up in one room and then drops them in another—his toys are everywhere!"

SOLUTION

Accept that your son will always be more likely than other children to move his toys—and some of yours—about the house, but minimize the migration by designating acceptable play areas.

Toys should not take over every corner of the house; it does children a disservice to teach them that their activities and interests take precedence over the activities and interests of others. Parents may be mistakenly led into believing that a home overrun with toys is a child-friendly home, but the ultimate goal should be a *family*-friendly home that promotes consideration for others, not selfishness.

To make your home family friendly, teach your child that toys must be corralled in the playroom. This may be a basement, an over-the-garage bonus room, a converted living room or dining room, a bedroom, or one end of the family room. Corralling toys into concrete play areas enables an ADD child, whose distraction might make him appear less considerate, to chip in at cleanup and alleviate that unfair impression of selfishness. Dividing the playroom into even smaller areas, like "play kitchen" and "train area," lets you assign more manageable cleanup projects to your ADD child. Instead of overwhelming him with the task of cleaning up an unsightly playroom, you can instead ask him to clean up just the train area.

Toy Mismanagement

PROBLEM

"The last owner installed beautiful custom cabinets in what is now our basement playroom. This makes plenty of room for all the toys, but somehow the cabinets are always empty and the toys are all over the floor."

SOLUTION

Ignore that beautiful, but non-ADD-appropriate custom cabinetry and procure cheap open shelving and some open-front bins or lidless clear tubs in which to store your children's toys.

For children, cleanup must be a quick, easy one-step process. Opening a cabinet door is just one step too many for any child, much less a child with ADD. Open shelves—uncrowded and outfitted with open-front bins and clear lidless tubs—are the simplest method for easy "wing it in" cleanup. Do not bother labeling bins: As long as they are clear, your children will be able to determine which is for what. And finally, embrace the key benefit of having a hidden basement playroom—close the door and hide the mess.

Within the playroom itself, specific play activities should all have their own nearby storage solutions for ADD-child-friendly cleanup. For instance, the large toy kitchen appliances go together in one corner to create a play kitchen. A **discrete** number of play food items and dishes can be stored in a clear open tub on top of the play fridge.

Open-front bins and clear open plastic tubs on shelves provide an easy target during cleanup. Stuffed animals and large collections have been reduced to a number that not only easily fits in the available storage, but also conforms to a manageable number for an ADD child to pick up.

Simple Rules for Toy Storage

- Provide *open* shelving in the play area.

- Never store toys in front of or stacked on top of each other.

- Each category of toy should have its own shelf or bin.

- Trucks, dolls, and stuffed animals should be lined up on shelves, not dumped in large toy boxes that take up useful floor space.

- Use shallow, clear bins to corral, without obscuring, collections of toys on shelves.

- Use open-front bins for easy access to collections of toys on shelves.

- Every toy in a bin should be visible at a single glance; if you have to rummage or dump to locate a toy, then reduce the collection.

- Some toys will require more than one bin. For instance, Barbies may require a clothing bin *and* an accessory tray for little shoes and other accessories.

- Avoid plastic drawers; they can be awkward to open.

- Avoid open mesh containers like milk crates—small items fall through.

- Avoid overloading children with too many toys or large collections of a particular type of toy.

Scheduling Cleanup Time

Children with ADD can have difficulty with transitions, and most thrive on routine. Make cleanup time a defined part of your *daily* routine. You will need to break tasks down—clean up the trucks, rather than clean up the room—and stay in the room to provide focus for your child. For this reason, schedule toy cleanup for a time when you are not distracted by other duties. Do not attempt to supervise cleanup while you are prepping dinner—leave it until after the dinner dishes are done.

If your spouse comes home at a regular time, schedule cleanup so that it is finished right when he or she walks through the door. That way your spouse can provide your child with immediate positive feedback: "Wow! The trucks are all picked up! I'm very proud of you!" Instant gratification is vital for ADD children.

An ADD child cannot manage the maintenance for large collections of toys. Do not sabotage him with an unwieldy, unnecessary, and probably unappreciated thirty action figures, when he can manage to play with and clean up only two.

Toy Collecting

The ADD daughter of a former client fell in love with the first book from a series called *The Boxcar Children.* This child eagerly anticipated school library day so that she could check out the second and then the third book. Her mother, who also battled with ADD, went out and bought every Boxcar book published (at that time more than forty books!). Although this was done out of love, forty-some books is an overwhelming reading list for anyone, never mind a child with ADD. An eagerly anticipated and joyful treat had thus been transformed into a discouraging and burdensome obligation.

The lesson here: Avoid comprehensive collections that can overwhelm your child and take the novelty out of a special toy. Remember that your child has only two hands, so how many race cars/Beanie Babies/books can he possibly hold? Usually it is the parent's perfectionistic need to "complete the collection" that drives this over-accumulation—not the needs of the child.

Overcrowded Play Areas

The ADD mother of two hyperactive sons and a toddler daughter asked for my help in organizing her basement playroom. This room had been outfitted with a series of expensive and space-consuming toys, including a folding Ping-Pong table, a full-size pinball machine, a convertible air hockey/foosball table, a low train table, a low Lego table, some large plastic kitchen appliances (stove, fridge, etc.), a free-standing puppet theater, a large plastic dollhouse, and a TV with a game box. Finally, an oversized sofa was placed along one wall, and a large treadmill was angled into a corner facing the TV.

Although this may sound like a child paradise equaled only by Disney World, the room was, in truth, a complete disaster as a playroom. Every playroom needs an open area for dance performances, wrapping paper roll sword fights, racetrack setup, temporary forts, and other active, creative play. This one provided no open space for a couple of hyperactive boys to tumble, horse around, and work off their energy during the long winter months and on rainy days. After some prodding, the mother donated some of the larger play items that the boys had outgrown and kept only the air hockey/foosball table. She moved the treadmill to the back of the basement and created an open area for active play.

Make a rule that racetracks and forts must come down at the end of the day. Otherwise, your children will leave them there and then co-opt other areas of your home for their play items.

Toy Purging

PROBLEM

"I am running out of space for my sons' toys, and neither boy is much good at cleaning up."

SOLUTION

You are not running out of space, you just have too many toys. The toy inventory needs to match the available storage space for toys within the playroom and needs to be reduced to a level the children can manage. If your child has to shift things around in order to put his toys away, then those toys are never going to leave the floor.

Purging toys is an ongoing job requiring highly sophisticated tactics: All children have closure issues on toys, and ADD children can become particularly attached to their favorites, taking comfort in the familiar. Yet it is not in their best interest to keep every broken, abandoned, or used toy. Go through your boys' room looking for items that get little use and put them in a bag near the front door for immediate donation. Continue purging until you have enough storage space to fit their toy inventory.

Before Christmas and birthdays, ask your child if he has any toys he would like to give to poor children. Whatever he gives you—punctured basketball included—praise him, and then quickly whisk the items out of sight so that he is not reminded of the loss.

Tender Tactics for Reduction

- **Hand-me-downs and giveaways.** Do not hang on to old toys for yard sales, cousins, or younger neighbors. It is inefficient to get rid of each toy in a different way and it's difficult for young children to see their former possessions in the hands of another. Instead, identify a convenient charity (one you drive by often) and use it for all of your child's stuff. Toys that are identified for donation immediately go into a discretely opaque garbage bag and then are thrown into the front seat of the car.

  Do let your children see all the other items in the house you regularly donate; make charitable donation and healthy closure a part of their upbringing. Hopefully by the time they are preteens, the family culture of charitable donation should be so ingrained that they begin to identify charity-appropriate items as they clean their rooms.

- **Involving your children.** Before Christmas and birthdays, ask your child if he has any toys he would like to give to poor children. Whatever he gives you—punctured basketball included—praise him, and then quickly whisk the items out of sight so that he is not reminded of the loss. This way, you are teaching him the value of charitable donation and making him more comfortable with closure.

When your young child is out of the house (or asleep), review the toys in his room along with the ones he has decided to donate. Put all of the best items into one opaque bag for donation and place all of the old and broken toys in another opaque bag for the trash. Don't worry that you will throw out something precious—you are his parent; you know what he loves and what he plays with regularly.

It is not necessary to tell your kids what you donated and trashed—you can't expect a level of generosity from your children that is developmentally inappropriate. As a parent, it is your job to do what is in your children's best interests (maintaining a clean and organized home), and to shield them from information that they are not yet ready to handle.

- **Prevention.** Neither an ADD parent nor an ADD child has the focus to manage too many toys. Limit the number of toys and create a playroom in which storage is so convenient and simple that your child can clean it up in minutes. Accomplishment, self-reliance, self-respect, and a generous nature are more precious gifts than plastic.

  Guard against over-gifting: Instead of inviting thirty children to your child's birthday party, invite his age plus one (so, for example, an eight-year-old gets to invite nine guests). For sleepover parties, invite half that number.

CHAPTER 8

The Bathroom

The bathroom is the first challenge of the day for someone with ADD. Managing the products and supplies required to get through your morning routine in a timely fashion is probably the first blow to your schedule. Efficiently cycling the no-longer-needed items out of the bathroom, while providing convenient storage for only those items that are used in the bathroom, may give you a chance to get ready and get out of the house on time.

Every bathroom in an ADD home should contain a **large** kitchen-sized garbage can for empty bottles, rejected products, packaging, expired medications, and used cotton balls and face wipes.

Coping with Limited Bathroom Space

PROBLEM

"I have lots to do before I get out in the morning, but my bathroom space is really small, so there's no room for all my stuff. I knock things over and it takes me forever to get ready."

Any toiletry item that you use daily should be left out on the counter next to the sink.

SOLUTION

Do less. Re-examine the need for all your lotions, creams, extensive daily makeup regimens, and aftershaves. Whittle down your products to make more space. Simplify your routine if possible: Reducing a 45-minute beauty routine to 10 minutes will help you get out of the house more easily.

Organize your daily essentials in a small bathroom with little built-in storage by leaving them out in the open. Any toiletry item that you use daily should be left out on the counter next to the sink. A plastic basket—with slotted sides for ventilation—is the perfect tool for holding all of your daily supplies. That way, you can scoop everything inside it when you need to clean the bathroom sink. Don't worry about emptying the basket afterward; things will migrate out on their own.

Basic Bathroom Organizing Tips

- A complete set of bathroom cleaning supplies and a roll of paper towels should be kept in or near the bathroom. Every toilet deserves its own toilet bowl brush.

- If you disrobe in the bathroom before you shower, add a tall laundry basket to use as a hamper.

- Get rid of that small decorative bathroom wastebasket (it's inefficient because it needs constant emptying) and replace it with a tall uncovered garbage can.

- Keep a box of baby wipes on the back of your toilet or a tub of disinfecting wipes near your counter for quick swipe-and-go cleanings.

- Consider hiring a cleaning service for your bathrooms and floors.

The ADD Girl's Bathroom

PROBLEM

"My ADD teen shares a bathroom with her non-ADD sister, who complains of things left soaking in the sink."

SOLUTION

Congratulate yourself that you have at least managed to get your ADD daughter to soak items in the sink, rather than leave them stained and crumpled on the floor. Now you just need to give her an easy, convenient alternative so that when she can't manage to finish the job, her sister will not be confronted with an unpleasant task in order to use the sink. A small plastic tub, like a lidless baby wipes tub, should live next to the sink, readily available for soaking duty. Yes, there will still occasionally be an unpleasant view near the sink, but at least no one need clear anything from the sink in order to brush her teeth.

ADD teens need to be brought along a step at a time; compromises must be made and squeamishness must bow to efficiency and reality. In a house of teen daughters, for example, feminine hygiene supplies should not be kept hidden in the back of a cabinet several feet away from the toilet but out in the open on a shelf within easy reach of the toilet. If the men in the family can stand to see these boxes on the aisle of the drugstore, then they can learn to live with them in the family bathroom.

The Overcrowded Medicine Cabinet

PROBLEM

"I got fed up with things tumbling out of my medicine closet and sorted them into black plastic tubs. It looks nice, but now I can't find anything."

SOLUTION

Throw out the tubs and replace them with open-front bins that allow you to see your medications at a glance. As you make the transfer, throw out anything that you never use, don't use anymore, or has expired. Be sure to have a large garbage bag handy for this chore; you will be amazed by the number of items that have expired! Even sunscreen and lotions have expiration dates.

Purchase only those medications targeted for your current or regular ailments. If you have a bad back and pop ibuprofen like candy, then by all means purchase an economy-sized jar, but don't buy the jar just because it's on sale and you might one day need it. Remember, you are not the drugstore; you don't have the space, money, or time to manage pharmaceutical stock.

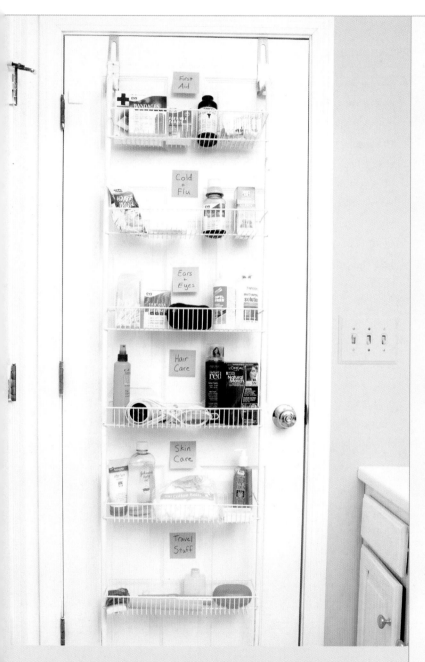

First
Aid

Cold
+
Flu

Ears
+
Eyes

Hair
Care

Skin
Care

Travel
Stuff

A wire rack on the back of the bathroom door provides storage for medicines and toiletries. Shelves are named like the aisles of a drugstore, and inventory reduced to conform to the available storage. Brightly colored sticky notes label the shelves until the system is memorized.

How to Organize a Medicine Cabinet or Closet

- Bring a large lawn-sized garbage bag up to the bathroom.

- Procure *open-front* bins and give them loose names, like the aisles of the drugstore: cold/flu bin, skin care bin, eye/ear/nose bin.

- Transfer medications and toiletries into these bins, throwing out the old, unused, unwanted, and expired items. Do not overstuff these bins, or your view will again be obscured!

- If you don't have a medicine closet, but rather an inadequate medicine chest, you may need to hang a wire-style spice rack behind the bathroom door for added storage. Give each shelf of the rack a rough name (label them until you have them memorized) and then keep your inventory down so that you don't overcrowd any one shelf.

- In the future, when a bin or shelf becomes crowded, go through just that bin or shelf and get rid of lesser-used and expired items.

Wet Towels

PROBLEM

"My teenage son who has ADD just leaves his towels on the floor in a wet heap. I keep reminding him to hang them over the towel bar to dry, but he doesn't."

SOLUTION

Reduce the number of towels in your home and simplify towel storage. Assign all family members two bath towels in colors that match their bedroom. Metal, over-the-door hooks can be purchased at any hardware store so that all family members can store their towels on the back of their bedroom door. Your son is never going to return to the bathroom in order to carefully spread a towel out over a towel bar to dry. However, if a hook is conveniently located in his bedroom, he just might drop his towel on it. I also recommend a couple of hooks in the bathroom for those who like to shed their towels and switch to their bathrobes in the bathroom.

Consequences are as important for ADD teens as for everyone else, so do not rescue your son with a clean towel when he leaves his old one in a heap on the floor. Let him use that soggy, grubby towel for his next several showers but enable him to fix the situation by providing him with the door hook. I guarantee he will soon learn to hang up his towels after a shower. By providing consequences, you will teach him a valuable life skill, cut down on your laundry, and give him a system that will reduce *his* laundry when he eventually lives on his own.

Every bathroom needs a tall, lidless laundry hamper for towels that are irredeemably dirty as well as cast-off pre-shower clothing.

Reduce the number of towels in your home and simplify towel storage. Assign all family members two bath towels in colors that match their bedroom.

The Problem with Toilet Paper Holders

I really would like to meet up with the bonehead who first inflicted the metal spring toilet paper holder upon our society. I have a spitball with his name on it for every time one of those springs jumped from my hand to either roll into an obscure location or plop into the toilet bowl. The simplest method for dispensing toilet paper is to put half a dozen rolls into a basket on the shelf next to your toilet. For us unhappy souls who do not possess a window ledge, radiator top, or counter within easy reach of the throne, I recommend the "arm-style" bar holder that mounts to your wall or stands on its own. You just slip the roll on—no disassembly/reassembly required.

Toilet paper rolls slip on and off this dispenser in one easy motion. Storage for extra rolls below cuts down on the number of times one must re-stock from the twelve-pack stored under the sink.

CHAPTER 9

The Office

In this day and age, everyone needs an office. Our schedules are too active, our bills too numerous, our taxes too complex, and our calendars too full to forgo an area devoted to paperwork. People with ADD, however, tend to trail their paperwork around the house. Unfortunately, this makes for a cripplingly inefficient system. When it comes time to fill out a form, pay a bill, or mail a letter, the relevant paperwork is never in the same room or rooms as the checkbook, stamps, and address book.

The Wandering Office

PROBLEM

"I like to do my paperwork on the couch and in bed, but that means that there are papers all over my apartment."

SOLUTION

Start by creating an office space that is as comfortable, or almost as comfortable, to work in as your couch or your bed. Identify one area of your home that can support a well-padded rolling chair and a usable desk. Although the chair is not as comfortable as the bed, it's easier to write on a desk than on your knees or a low coffee table. Now that you have a more comfortable working space, gather and move *all* of your paperwork—active, reference, projects, bills, taxes, archival, calendar, and mail to that one area. Supply the area with a reasonable number of stationery supplies so that paperwork processing is efficient and stress free. Make sure that your work area is also equipped with bright lighting, a phone, and a padded chair, so the office itself becomes a comfortable, and even desirable, place to work. The truth is, even after all of this, you may never completely confine your paperwork to the office. But if the office is well-lit, conveniently arranged, and comfortable, and if it contains all of the materials you need to process paperwork, then you'll be more likely to do your work there.

Outfitting the Office

For a comfortable and efficient office space, you'll need the following:

- A desk with at least one drawer for stationery supplies
- A *comfortable* rolling desk chair
- Bright lighting—both a desk lamp and an overhead bulb are desirable
- A two-drawer file cabinet within arm's reach of the desktop

In your stationery drawer:

- Tape, stapler, staples, a pad of paper, paper clips, rubber bands, stamps, envelopes, and one pack of multicolored manila file folders

On your desktop:

- A computer
- Stacking trays
- A pencil holder with retractable pens, a few pencils, scissors, and red and black felt-tip markers for creating files or drawing attention to items on your calendar
- A phone, phone book, and address book
- A calendar
- An electric pencil sharpener

And most important, within arm's reach of your desk:

- A wastebasket and tall recycling basket
- A small television or radio, if you like to work to those

Keep no more than six files in a filing cabinet drawer.

A comfortable chair entices one into using the office rather than the bed or the couch. A tall and convenient recycling basket encourages easy "one pile" filing. A single drawer holds enough stationary supplies. Stacking trays, in varied colors, organize piles of papers vertically.

Creating an ADD-Friendly Work Space

How does the desk pictured here suit someone with ADD? Here are some of the tricks that make this an ADD-friendly work space:

- Stationery essentials fit together in one drawer—it's inefficient to both manage a large inventory and wander the house hunting down supplies.

- Only retractable pens are included, which eliminates the distraction of playing with caps.

- Randomly colored folders (not to be confused with color-coded folders) act as a quick visual reminder for finding papers.

- Stackable trays allow you to file without opening a drawer and hunting down a folder.

- A handy wastebasket encourages you to throw out garbage the minute you are done with it.

- A recycling basket encourages you to throw out those questionable papers that might be garbage, because you know you could retrieve them before recycling day if you had to.

Paper-Filing Fiasco

PROBLEM

"I never use my file drawers; everything is just stacked on my desk, but this leaves me without a place to work."

SOLUTION

Make your stacking system work for you by utilizing stacking trays. It is almost as easy to shove something in a stacking tray as on a pile, and stacking trays keep paperwork out and visible, the way you probably like it.

Use your stacking trays so that each one counts as a file folder category. This may require a couple of fairly tall towers of stacking trays, so pile them high but make sure you can still comfortably see and reach inside. As an aid to memory, mix up the colors of the trays. Clear plastic in bright colors is best, but black, clear, and beige will also do. Lay a brightly colored file folder on the bottom of each tray for use as a label, and use a felt-tipped pen to print the name of the tray category on the file tab so it can easily be seen.

Now, instead of stacking your papers haphazardly on your desktop, you can spend about the same amount of effort shoving them in the appropriate stacking tray, and you won't feel as overwhelmed by that one tall pile. You will still have a piling system, but that system will be up off your desk, and the piles themselves will be segregated by category and labeled.

Basket Case

A single tray impedes access to all but the top most papers, and devolves from an Active Paperwork tray into an ever-growing pile of neglected, dated and random papers.

"I never go through my Active Paperwork tray—the stack is now so tall that I just go ahead and pile new papers on my desktop."

A slender upright Active Paperwork basket allows easy access to all papers, and encourages weeding of the old and dated. As the Active Paperwork basket is located near a phone, it also holds the address book.

Trade your tray for an upright Active Paperwork basket. You will be able to flip through your upright active paperwork more easily, as every piece will be accessible, and you will be more likely to weed as you go. Make sure the basket isn't too large; you want to make it small enough that you are forced to go through it once a month or so to weed out the old and obsolete.

Any mail that needs to be discussed with a spouse or family member (are we going to this wedding?), or any form that needs to be immediately filled out and mailed should just be left out in front of the basket as a visual reminder to have this conversation or fill out this form today.

File Weeding

PROBLEM

"I dread going through my files. I avoid it and the papers just continue to accumulate."

SOLUTION

You can greatly simplify the dreaded file-weeding process by discarding whole files instead of papers. Go through your files folder by folder (or tray by tray). If a project is old or complete, throw out the whole file *without looking inside it* until you have six or fewer files per cabinet drawer. Whenever you create a new file folder, pick a bright color to make it immediately distinguishable.

Do *not* group files by color, such as making all home repair files green and all tax returns blue. Group them only by location in the file drawer, but make each individual file a different color so that when you are in the home repair section of the drawer, you can easily distinguish your outdoor projects from your plumbing estimates.

To simplify file weeding in the future, save fewer papers. Unless you have identified an imminent use for a piece of paper, dump it in the recycling basket next to your desk (you can always retrieve it if you have to). This way, you're weeding your files as you go. Do not save papers for a possible future project. Rest assured that you will be able to gather that information—fresh—should you ever wish to begin that project.

Stop saving unnecessary papers. Statistics show that people retrieve only about 20 percent of what they file. For someone with ADD, this wasted space, visual clutter, and unneeded filing effort interfere with efficiency.

Papers that need to be regularly accessed for ongoing projects and activities (including bills that need to be accessed for the project of "paying them") should each have their own activity or project file tray.

Extra Tips for Paperwork Management

- In revising your file system, keep to those valuable precepts—reduction of materials (papers), reduction of steps (stacking trays over drawers), and efficiency before beauty (random colored files)—that will simplify your paperwork.

- Don't be seduced by the mechanical labeler with its bewitching uniform labels. Yes, they are easy to read and look neat on a folder, but they are just too time consuming. When you take into account the data entry, peeling and positioning, label refilling, and battery replacement involved, it's just quicker and easier to grab a felt-tipped pen and write your label by hand.

- If you find yourself lugging paperwork between work and home or your paperwork is inevitably spread throughout the house, keep all paperwork categorized in a *single* flex folder with dividers. This way, your paperwork is portable and organized in one location. Plus, a single folder forces an occasional weeding before things get too overwhelming.

Location, Location, Location

Paperwork falls into four categories: Archival, Reference/Projects, Active, and Wastepaper. While it's best if you can keep all of your paperwork in the same general location next to your phone and calendar, you may want to target more specific locations for each type of paperwork:

Archival Paperwork

Tool: A file drawer

Location: In your office in a remote file drawer

Contents: A bottom file drawer should accommodate those archival materials you must keep but that you will probably rarely or never need to touch again: seven years only of tax returns, your Dad's death certificate, your marriage license, etc. Even here, though, some weeding should be done; when you add this year's tax return, throw out the one from eight years ago.

Reference/Projects Paperwork

Tool: Upright stacking trays

Location: Near your calendar or in your office

Contents: Papers that need to be regularly accessed for ongoing projects and activities (including bills that need to be accessed for the project of "paying them") should each have their own activity or project file tray. For example, the religious school curriculum handbook goes in the Synagogue tray; the soccer league guidelines go in the Sports tray; paint chips and fabric swatches belong in the Family Room Remodeling Project tray; hotel brochures go in the Vacation Planning Project tray, etc. At the end of the soccer season or remodeling project, throw out the entire contents of the tray.

Keep a checkbook, envelopes, pen, and stamps near the area where you sort mail so that bills (and other mail) can either be dealt with the moment they arrive or tossed into the bill-paying project tray, where they can gather until bill paying day.

Active Papers

Tool: An upright basket

Location: Near the phone and calendar

Contents: These are papers that describe upcoming events, pertain to immediate scheduling, or give information for immediate action items on your "to do" lists. Invitations for events that you are planning to attend, the starting address for this weekend's road race, this month's church bulletin, and the Web link to the bridal registry so you can order a gift all go into an upright Active basket. The one or two papers—field trip permission form, phone message from a client—that need to be attended to within 24 to 48 hours should lay on the counter or desktop in front of your Active basket to keep them on your "urgent" radar.

Keep your upright Active basket small so that you are forced to weed through it just about monthly. As active papers have an immediate expiration date, most of the basket's contents can be tossed out within thirty days.

Wastepaper

Tool: Wastepaper basket and recycling bin

Location: Multiple—under your desk, next to where you sort the mail, next to your calendar, and next to every phone

Contents: Wastepaper includes junk mail, paid bills, catalogs, greeting cards, invitations for past events, and anything else that's useless or outdated. Shred and discard anything that has your Social Security number on it and/or your credit card number. These shreds should then be put in the garbage (so they are sealed) rather than the recycling bin.

Managing the Mail

PROBLEM

"My husband comes in and dumps the mail on the kitchen counter—I cannot get him to walk it over to the office. He even starts to answer the mail on the counter, but then leaves it half done. And I can't pick up the mail and move it without messing up his system!"

If you must sort mail in the kitchen, do it near the kitchen phone and Active Paperwork basket. This way, your invitations can get an immediate RSVP by phone, and once the date is marked on the calendar, they can be placed into the Active Paperwork basket for later reference regarding directions.

SOLUTION

A mail-sorting center in the kitchen, near the phone, includes stacking trays, a recycling bin, and a garbage can. Envelopes, a low wire basket for stamps, a checkbook and a discrete inventory of stationary supplies support on-the-spot processing.

Create a mail-sorting center in a convenient corner of the kitchen, near where he is dumping the mail, but separate from cooking activities. You may never get your husband to walk into the next room, but you may be able to nudge him over a few feet and encourage him to sort the bulk of the mail up off the counter if you create a more efficient and convenient system.

Set up a tower or two of stacking trays to create a mail-staging area. Place a colored file folder on the bottom of each tray with the category (bills, statements, or charity) clearly written on the tab. If possible, place these trays near the Active Paperwork basket/calendar because many items, such as invitations and information about events, will go directly into the Active basket. When the mail comes in, your husband can easily scan each piece and fling it into the appropriate tray. Set a garbage can and recycling bin next to the stacking trays so that junk mail—the largest volume of everyone's mail—can go *directly* into the garbage bin during the sort. On bill-paying day, scoot the bills, statements, and charities stacks out of their trays and move them into the office. If your husband prefers to deal with bills on the spot, the mail-staging area should be equipped with a checkbook, stamps, mailing labels, and pens. Once you and your husband both get used to this new and improved mail-management system, you'll be able to move the mail without creating any problems or confusion.

Mail Support Items

The top tray of your new mail-sorting center or the counter next to the trays should hold the following office supplies so that, when appropriate, mail can be processed on the spot and then put in front of the door to go out the next day:

- A pen
- A pad of paper
- A checkbook
- Envelopes
- Address labels
- Stamps
- A few paper clips

Be sure to define and then use your mail area as a separate and segregated center from the meal-prep area—papers and food **do not** mix.

Bill-Paying Backlog

PROBLEM

"I don't have that many bills, but I dread bill paying. Sometimes, even though I have plenty of money, my credit card gets refused or my utilities get cut off."

SOLUTION

Reduce the number of bills you pay, and make the process of bill paying efficient and convenient so that it feels quick and comfortable rather than dreadful. Here are some suggestions for easing the pain of paying bills:

- Rely on automatic recurring payments whenever possible. If you have to, switch to a bank that offers the option of online bill paying or automatic recurring debits.

- Cut up all of your credit cards except one Visa or MasterCard and one American Express. Use only one of the cards and keep the other as a backup. This should get your credit card bills down to one a month.

- Wherever possible (the gas station, the grocery store), use your debit rather than your credit card so that the intermediary step of bills can be eliminated completely.

- By all means give to charity, but give large sums infrequently (once a month or less) to a single charity rather than small sums all of the time to a variety of causes. This will reduce the number of checks you need to track for tax deduction.

- Equip your bill-paying area with stamps, envelopes, your checkbook, pens, and address labels so you can pay bills in one fell swoop.

- And finally, make sure your bill-paying area is welcoming and comfortable enough that you'll want to use it: Add a comfy rolling chair.

Don't waste time filing paperwork for paid bills. **Throw out paid bill invoices the moment you pay the bills.** If you ever really need to go back and question anything—if you one day decide to compare water rates from one year to the next—then rest assured that the water department, credit card company, and power company are all keeping those records for you, and they're only a phone call away.

Financial Statement Backlog

PROBLEM

"The brokerage house sends me a free three-ring binder for organizing all my nicely hole-punched financial statements, but I am still years behind in filing my financial statements."

File your financial statements by tossing them in a box. This way they will instantly be filed in chronological order.

SOLUTION

You aren't using the binder system because it is ridiculously inconvenient and time consuming. Switch to the easier system of filing your statements in a box (bank statements with cancelled checks in a small box, large investment reports in a bigger box). Simply wing your statements into the appropriate box as soon as you receive them in the mail. This way, financial reports will automatically be filed in chronological order. You may wish to write the date, boldly and in marker, on the front of the envelope for easy reference. When a box gets full enough, stand the statements on end so that you can more easily flip through them. After 18 months or so, throw out any old bank statements and cancelled checks.

Unfortunately, in years past, brokerage houses and investment firms did not give a year-end summary of purchases, so that all statements needed to be kept for declaring capital gains when assets were eventually sold. Today, however, most financial houses give a year-end summary of purchases along with their 1099-DIVs and 1099-Ints. This, then, is all you need to keep on hand.

Bank statements are kept in their envelopes and stored in a box to create a de-facto chronological filing system. When the box gets full enough, stand the statements upright so it is easier to flip through them.

Tax Forms

The one form of paperwork you will need to keep is year-end income reviews and deductions. Get rid of your pay stubs (after a quick check that the withholdings look about right), but keep your W2. Dump your credit card bill (tear it up first), but save any that include a charitable donation and wing these into your Tax Deduction tray or folder. Toss your cancelled checks, but again, first go through them and remove any charitable donations for your Tax Deduction tray or folder.

Magazine and Catalog Control

PROBLEM

"How can I organize my food magazines so that I can find the recipes I want? I paid a professional to help me set up an indexing system, but I could never keep up with it, and now I am years behind even **reading** them, and the stacks next to my bed are overflowing."

SOLUTION

Stop attempting to index. Instead, cancel your subscriptions to all but one weekly magazine and one monthly magazine, and then donate your entire backlog to the public library or, if the pictures are pretty, to the local elementary school art department. From here on in, when a new magazine arrives, throw out the old one whether you've read it or not. Yes, I know that valuable and irreplaceable recipes, knitting patterns, garden designs, and decor ideas will be lost to your immediate convenience, but really how convenient have they been sitting under a pile by your bedside? If you follow the "one in/one out rule," then you will never have more than two magazines in your home at any one time, and magazine storage should never become an issue.

Those who suffer from ADD do not have the time or patience to save, file, and index every article that comes into their homes on the off chance they may some day need to know how to incorporate an intarsia cable pattern into a baby sweater. This is the job of the public library—providing shelves, staff, indexing systems, and maintenance to relieve this burden from the average citizen.

If you really want more than one weekly magazine subscription and one monthly subscription, purchase another as a gift to the local public library so that you can enjoy them at will without having to index and shelve them in your home.

Magazine and Catalog Control

Stacking blocks access to all but the top most magazines and makes is difficult and unwieldy to remove older issues.

> **Never stack your magazines—it prevents access to all but the top few.**

Reducing the number of subscriptions and storing the remaining magazines upright makes it easy to flip through and weed out older issues.

Tips for Magazine Storage

If you live in a home where multiple family members receive and share magazines, or if you save up catalogs by season (all the winter gardening catalogs are retained until the spring seed order, for example), then you will need to impose a magazine storage system.

- Store magazines where they are read. The "Big Three" areas for magazine perusal are the living room couch, the bedside table, and the toilet.

- Store your magazines in an upright rack so that you can easily see every magazine as you flip through. Newer magazines go to the front, so you can easily weed out the older issues in the back of the rack.

- Use a small magazine rack to encourage you to keep magazines to a minimum.

- Never stack your magazines—it prevents access to all but the top few.

- Never overstuff your magazine rack—what good is it to own magazines if you have to wrestle them in and out of the rack?

If you haven't ordered anything from a catalog after a month, throw it out and congratulate yourself for saving money on something you probably didn't need all that urgently anyway.

When to Save Catalogs

The great thing to remember about catalogs is that they are advertisements. Toss them out for good unless they belong in one of the following two categories:

- If you have been awaiting a specific catalog—the Lands' End swimsuit catalog, for example—then by all means remove it from the mail and either flip through it or put it in your Active basket for imminent perusal. If you haven't ordered anything from it after a month, throw it out and congratulate yourself for saving money on something you probably didn't need all that urgently anyway.

- If you need to collect several catalogs for, let's say, a gardening project you are working on, store them in your magazine rack or in a project stacking tray on your desktop until the project is complete, then throw them out.

All other catalogs get thrown *immediately* into recycling.

"The Strikers"
Indoor Soccer Game Schedule
Winter 2006

Date	Home/away	Shirt color	field	time	Team captain
1/7	home	blue	Kennedy High school	11:00	Russell
1/14	away	white	Merritt Indoor sports	2:00	Michael
1/21	home	blue	Kennedy High	12:30	Joey
1/28	home	blue	Kennedy High	10:00	Alex
2/4	away	white	Washington Highs	9:30	David
2/11	away	white	Reilly Arena	2:00	Robert
2/18	away	white	Whittaker Rec	11:30	Seth
2/13 tournament		To be announced	Olympia Stadium	9:00	Richard
2/25	away	white	Lawrence Tech	3:00	Matt
3/4/	home	blue	Kennedy High	10:00	Bill
Play-offs			TBA	TBA	

Coach Jim Green
555-1212
CoachGreen@soccer.org

Hockey Game Schedule
Jan-March
Team Captain Jim Leary 555-4545

Date	Home/away	Shirt color	field
1/6	home	red	Park Rink
1/13	away	black	Olympia Stadium
1/20	home	red	Park Rink
1/27	home	red	Park Rink
2/3	away	black	Merritt Indoor
2/10	away	black	Reilly Arena
2/17	away	black	Lawrence Tech
2/24 tournament		To be announced	
3/3	away	black	Whittaker Rec
3/10	home	red	Park Rink
Play-offs			TBA

June 2006

Sunday	Monday	Tuesday	Wednesday	Thursday	Friday	Saturday
				1	2	3 — Patches to vet 10:00
4	5	6 — Lisa to Dr. 9:00	7	8	9	10
11	12	13	14	15 — dinner with Claire 7:00	16	17
18	19	20	21	22	23	24
25	26 — P.T.O. Meeting 7:00	27	28	29	30	

CHAPTER 10

Calendars and Scheduling

The myriad interests, ceaseless enthusiasm, and impulsivity of people with ADD often lead them to overcommit, while their lack of patience often prevents them from working out details and following through on plans. The most realistic and effective approach to this innate problem is *not* finding a way to juggle an overcommitted schedule, nor is it using a complicated calendar system to record details and increase follow-through. Instead, scheduling the lives of those with ADD requires a reduction of steps and materials. Socially acceptable strategies for reducing commitments to a manageable level—learning to delegate responsibilities, share commitments, and gracefully decline invitations—need to be adopted, and at-a-glance calendars, which require no more effort to maintain than picking up a pen, must be employed.

Calendar Consolidation

PROBLEM

"I have a work calendar and a home calendar, and even though I try to sit down and update both regularly, something always gets missed."

SOLUTION

Reduce your calendars to one so that nothing need ever be transferred. A career person should have one calendar. That calendar should be kept in a purse or briefcase and should travel back and forth with you to home and work. It is just more efficient to keep one calendar.

This becomes a bit more complicated when you share your calendar with others. Although it is relatively easy to coordinate on a regular basis with one's spouse (ask your non-ADD spouse to take it upon himself or herself to ask you daily for any new scheduling information), a busy and active family will need a central and stationary family calendar that everyone can mark and reference.

Components of the Family Calendar

Even if you carry your one calendar with you, wait before committing to an appointment or event. Answer all invitations and obligations with, "Sounds good. Call me at home so I can check my desk/home calendar." This gives you a chance to review your schedule and think before you commit.

Family calendars need to accommodate three types of schedules:

- **The day-to-day schedule.** This should be marked with doctor appointments, lunch dates, and all other one-time events.

- **A permanent "matrix" that outlines the regular, recurring obligations of the family's week.** These might include: Sunday—all to Church, Mom—Friday night bingo, Jimmy—Thursday Cub Scouts, Jill—swim practice after school Mondays and Wednesdays, and Dad—Thursday poker nights.

- **Activity and seasonal schedules** These might be the baseball schedule that gives the location and shirt colors for each game (game times, if they varied, were written on the day-to-day calendar the moment the schedule was received), the Cub Scout schedule giving the snack rotation and prospective meeting agendas with supplies, the book group hostess rotation schedule, and so on.

The Importance of "To Do" Lists

A pencil holder and some bright pads of paper or *large*, 4" x 6"-sized, Post-Its should flank every phone in your home. These pads are not just for message taking; they are the "to do" lists and reminder notes that are conveniently located so you can catch your thoughts as they occur. Even if you leave the room without retrieving the list, you will have the memory of writing your thought down.

Naturally, it is best if you can remember to slap these reminders on, or in front of, the door or slip them in your pockets on the way out. Vary the color of pads from room to room so that you have an easy reference for which scrap of paper you are digging out of your pocket or purse (such as blue from the blue pad in the bedroom). The brighter the paper, the better these pads will work as a mnemonic reminder.

Start every morning with the day's "to do" list. Scrawl the day of the week on the paper pad next to your phone and jot down reminders of errands to be run, phone calls to be placed, and groceries to be bought. Place the list, not the whole pad, into your pocket or purse when you leave. At night, fish out this list to see if anything needs to be transferred to tomorrow's list. Be sure to use the day of the week as the title of each "to do" list. This makes it easier to identify the current list from those that are obsolete.

The daily "to do" list is also the shopping list.

Phone Support Items

The most oft-used one or two phones in your home should have a complete *but small* stationery supply, which should fit into a single stationery caddy:

- Four or five retractable pens
- Four or five pencils
- Pad of paper or 4" x 6" pad of sticky notes
- An eraser
- Pencil sharpener (or one nearby)
- One black and one red felt-tipped pen
- One pair of scissors
- One roll of tape
- One calculator
- A stapler

If the phone is in an office, add:

- Paper clips
- Rubber bands
- Multicolored file folders
- Tape and staples in your desk drawer

The Binder and Bulletin Board Methods

No matter which of the following methods you choose for your family calendar, you must keep it near the phone and the Active Paperwork basket. If at all possible, it should also be located in the same room as the computer and office.

1 **The binder method.** This method is best for someone who constantly runs the family calendar between the office and the kitchen. As long as the binder wanders no farther than these two rooms, you'll have an easy reference system for keeping track of upcoming activities.

- Procure a binder, a monthly 8" x 11" calendar that comes with three holes punched, and a package of clear plastic binder sleeves pre-punched with three holes.
- Insert the calendar into the front of the binder and put the clear sleeves together at the back.
- Create a "matrix" of your family's recurring activities by hand or on the computer by making a list of everyone's set weekly activities on a blank weekly calendar template. Place the matrix in the first plastic sleeve, and put that sleeve at the front fo the binder so that the matrix always faces the current month.

As old calendar months become obsolete, there is no need to unsnap the binder—the pages can just be ripped out.

- Place other schedules and rosters (the garbage recycling pick-up schedule, the school calendar) in the other plastic sleeves for easy reference.
- Keep the Active basket nearby for bulletins, newsletters, and other active scheduling paperwork. Keep some brightly colored felt pens nearby to mark the calendar as needed.

The binder method for scheduling includes a binder with the monthly calendar, a matrix of semi-permanent weekly activities, and individual activity schedules in plastic sleeves. Nearby, a stationary caddy holds a discrete number of stationary supplies. The Active Paperwork basket with address book; and the daily "to do" and groceries list are integral to the scheduling process. A wastepaper basket, though not shown, is conveniently located to the right.

- Introduce all family members to the family calendar and explain how it's used. Encourage them to mark their own events and appointments as they arise.

Your calendar is a great "to do" list. If you get an invitation, mark on the calendar when the RSVP should be sent in. If it's too early in the year to schedule a septic cleaning, while you are thinking of it, mark a day on your calendar several months hence when it would be appropriate to call.

2 **The bulletin board option.** The bulletin board calendar is best if you have space for it near your phone. It's less portable, but it allows you to see everything at one time without having to open a binder.

- Hang a regular, day-by-day calendar on a large bulletin board near your phone. (In this modern age of cell phones, almost any open wall space will do.)
- Tack any ancillary schedules next to the calendar on the same bulletin board.
- Attach a whiteboard and mark it up for use as the "matrix," or create a matrix on the computer and tack that next to the other schedules.

- Place your upright Active Paperwork basket near the bottom of the calendar.
- Make space nearby for pens, pencils, markers, etc.

How do you schedule appointments on a bulletin board calendar when you are out of the house? The correct answer is: You can't. After your dental appointment, ask the receptionist to give you a call later that day, when your calendar will be in front of you, to make your next appointment. Want to make a date with a friend? Ask her to call you at home to confirm. Put the onus for action on the other party to keep track of all upcoming events on a stationary calendar.

The bulletin board calendar uses a white board for the weekly matrix. The monthly calendar and activity schedules are pinned to the board. A clear upright bin affixed to the board holds active paperwork and a pad of paper for "to do" lists. A pencil holder corrals a discrete number of stationary supplies near a cell phone.

Overscheduled, Overcommitted, and Over Your Head

PROBLEM

"I am so busy that it's almost impossible for me to get everything done. I need a fail-proof, very sophisticated, ADD-friendly calendar system to keep it all straight. What system do you recommend?"

SOLUTION

I recommend that you use a simple one-calendar system—almost any kind will do—and then learn how to reduce your commitments. Complicated calendar and scheduling books that have "to do" lists; contain weekly, monthly, and yearly goal lists; or require punching through a series of computer menus to access your calendar are just too complex and inefficient to maintain. They eat up your valuable time in all those extra data entry steps. Instead, use a pad of paper next to your most commonly used phone as a daily "to do" list, and keep one calendar on a bulletin board, in a binder, or in a day planner—it really makes no difference. As long as you can quickly and efficiently get your schedule, goals, and action items marked down on *concrete dates,* your calendar will serve you rather than have you service it.

Keep pads of paper (and wastebaskets) and pencil jars in any room in which you spend a lot of time— not just near the phones.

Communication and Overcommitment

If you're like many people with ADD, you're an "idea person" who gets so enthusiastic about new projects that you overcommit to them before old projects have been completed. Employers and spouses can become irritated when a tumultuous improvement project or space has been left incomplete or unrestored while you move on to something else. While it's impossible to change your nature (nor should you—it is a valuable asset to the company or family), you can learn how to use honesty, delegation, and professional help to enable your employer or spouse to feel less frustrated and more empowered in the process.

First things first: When you realize that you are overscheduled, admit it. Everyone around you probably already knows that you've bitten off more than you can chew; better to leave them impressed with your honesty than frustrated by your avoidance. Here are several ways to carry out this conversation:

- **Overcommitted.** Just because you can fit something onto your calendar doesn't mean that you should. It is okay to say, "Technically I am available, but that weekend is so overcommitted that it wouldn't be wise to take on another obligation."

- **On second thought.** Do not be subject to the Tyranny of the Promise. It is perfectly acceptable—even mature and responsible—to admit that, in retrospect, you shouldn't have promised a trip to the ice cream stand after the 8:00 show, or to head up the new program before you had completed the program for the past fiscal year. Go ahead and tell your employer, friend, spouse, or even your children, "On second thought, I now realize that this plan or schedule is too tight or ambitious. I'm sorry to disappoint you, but it's just not realistic."

- **How can we make this work?** Once you've admitted that you are floundering, when appropriate, involve the other person in resolving the issue. Give them some options so they feel empowered. For example, "I can finish A if the deadline is extended; but if you need it imminently, it is more practical to assign it to someone else." In the home, suggest to your spouse, "Perhaps we can set aside a day when you can get me back on track by having the two of us tackle it together, or you can do it and I will take over the cooking this week," or "if you want, go ahead and hire a painter to complete the project."

- **Altogether.** To really wow them with your newfound sense of responsibility, admit to having overcommitted *and* suggest a practical solution to the problem:

1. Memorize a sincerely apologetic (but not self-deprecating) delivery of the following: "Upon reflection/study of my schedule, I realize that I am too overcommitted at this time to take on/complete this project and do it justice. Realistically, something has to give. Would you prefer to assign it to someone else/hire a professional or remove some of my other commitments so that I may focus my attention on this?"

2. When you realize that you have lost interest in a project and need to move on, a variant of this sentiment could be: "I have been reflecting on why I can't seem to get this done. I think we have to be realistic and realize that this follow-up work/implementation/cleanup is not my strength. I think it would be more efficient and practical to look into hiring someone, trading favors, assigning me a partner, or trading assignments in order to overcome the inertia surrounding this task and see it completed."

CHAPTER 11

Storage Spaces

In my travels through the basements, attics, and closets of the ADD community, I've seen the same mistake again and again: storage space filled to the bursting point in order to take the pressure off the rest of the house. My ADD clients are motivated to procure items for the home, but completely unmotivated to remove items from the home. Things that should never have been purchased in the first place, or that were once handy but are now no longer needed, linger in these remote storage areas while the client procrastinates disposing of them. By the time I arrive, it is impossible to walk through my clients' attics, basements, and garages without sidestepping the clutter. Even worse, the living areas have been invaded by items that should be stored away. The only way to reclaim your living spaces and bring order to your storage areas is to eliminate objects that are overstock or are no longer needed and create sensible and easily sustainable storage—shelves and hooks—for those possessions that remain.

The Unused Entry Hall Closet

PROBLEM

This lovely closet will never get used by the ADD family member who has no patience for time-consuming hangers and out of reach opaque baskets that force one to "guess the contents".

"My daughter seems incapable of walking across the hall to hang her coat in the coat closet—she just drops it on a chair next to the door. I have arranged baskets on the closet shelf for her to drop in her gloves, but she leaves her gloves on the chair as well."

SOLUTION

A low open basket to catch keys and gloves, and a coat rack next to the door for hat, jacket and purse just might be convenient enough to keep the ADD family member's possessions off the chairs, tables, and floor.

Your ADD family member is never going to walk across the hall, open the closet door, pull out a hanger, hang up her coat, and then pull down an attractive rattan bin to deposit her leather gloves therein. She instinctively feels that this is too much fuss and energy to spend on storing an item she will retrieve in less than twelve hours. People with ADD help us see how much valuable time we spend bowing to conventional methods. Your daughter knows that the coat closet makes sense only for her rarely used rain jacket, not for her everyday jacket and gloves. She also knows that a matching set of opaque baskets might be pretty, but it in no way aids us in storing, and may even hinder us in locating, our gloves.

To keep things neat, provide an acceptable and convenient method for her to store her coat next to the door. A hook on the wall or a coatrack next to the door where she usually drops her coat might be convenient enough to induce her to hang it up. A low table with a shallow basket next to the coatrack will provide a handy target in which to drop her keys and gloves. None of this will look as neat as a closed closet door, but it creates a system that might actually get used, and a jacket on a hook will always look better than a jacket on a chair.

Tips for Coat Storage

- No member of the family should own more than three coats—heavy winter, spring jacket, and trench/rain coat.

- If you have a large family and lots of coats to store, give the closet space to the non-ADD members of the family and provide hooks and shallow baskets on low tables directly next to the door for those who have ADD.

- If your ADD wife/husband/child continues to ignore the hook, place a large, attractive rattan basket next to a low table. She can dump her backpack and coat in this basket almost as easily as she can set them on the floor.

Basement Beautification

PROBLEM

"I have bought all sorts of boxes and tubs for my basement, but every time I need something, I have to go through all of the boxes, which then end up in the middle of the floor in a big pile. Can you give me a good labeling system?"

SOLUTION

Replace the boxes and opaque tubs with clear tubs so that labeling becomes unnecessary. And reduce the number of goods you are storing in the basement to those tubs and items that will fit onto shelves; I suggest flexible, modular plastic utility shelves. Items that are left on the floor—even when they are neatly arranged— give a stressful impression of clutter. These same items on a shelf give a restful impression of order. Why is that? We don't know, but it's one of the Great and Mysterious Laws of Organizing. Large tubs scattered all over your basement floor will feel stressful and, of course, are an inefficient waste of potential vertical storage space. Clear, unlabeled tubs placed on shelves (no stacking!) will give you a clear view of and easy access to your possessions.

The main purpose of your basement is *storage.* The greatest mistake clients make is finishing off their entire basement— eliminating most, if not all, of their rough storage—to make another living area. No house can remain uncluttered if all of the items that should live in the basement, like tools, seasonal decorations, and exercise equipment, have to be crammed into the main living areas.

Maintaining available empty shelving will help guard against allowing things to clutter up the floor.

The only way to reclaim your living spaces and bring order to your storage areas is to eliminate objects that are overstock or are no longer needed and create sensible and easily sustainable storage—shelves and hooks— for those possessions.

Basement Beautification Tips

- Never underestimate the value of a hook or nail. They can be handily driven into basement studs to hang items that require too much shelf space. Backpacks, pool nets, and heavy-duty extension cords are more appropriate for hanging on some nails or a hook than lying flat on shelves.

- Always maintain one or two empty shelves and unoccupied hooks in your basement for use as a staging area. You may need to store the prizes for the upcoming church bingo game, or the camping supplies for next week's Girl Scout camping trip.

- Give each activity and storage category its own area of the basement. Set up separate activity centers or storage spaces for your seasonal decorations, camping supplies, pet items, etc.

- It's much harder to keep a poorly lit basement organized. Anyone, in the course of an afternoon, can install cheap fluorescent lighting in a basement. Don't be too cheap, though; if you have 500 square feet in your basement, install a minimum of five fluorescent lights.

Christmas and Holiday Storage

PROBLEM

"I love Christmas, but my husband doesn't get everything put away until May, and then I still find bits of Christmas all over the house well into July."

SOLUTION

Reduce your Christmas inventory to increase your Christmas cheer. Your husband can't get Christmas cleaned up until May because he is overwhelmed by an inventory of Christmas decorations appropriate to adorn all of the workshops of the North Pole. Allow yourself one tall modular shelf of Christmas decorations, and then donate the rest. Even so, consider using the Big Christmas, Little Christmas model: One year purchase a small tree, use only one box of decorations on it, and call it a holiday. The next year, after your husband has had a chance to rest up and feel some Christmas nostalgia, go ahead and use all of the items from all of the boxes on your shelf.

Holiday decorations that don't get used on Big Christmas should be thrown out as too shabby or obsolete. That's right, just because cousin Joe made that Styrofoam snow flake in kindergarten forty years ago doesn't mean you need to keep it forever. As for those Christmas items that get found in July, forgive yourself; no one is perfect. Just keep one tub open and half full so that stragglers can easily be tossed inside, without order, as they appear.

Tips for a Happy Holiday

Families with an adult ADD member need to find ways of reducing chores around the holidays, not creating them. Try these useful tips to ensure a happier holiday:

- Do not allow your Christmas supplies to grow out of your Christmas shelf, and resist the American insanity of turning your house exterior into Santa's Village. String one set of lights on a bush, and use the time you've saved to see the Christmas displays downtown. In this way, you will have created a warm and happy Christmas memory rather than a marital spat and burdensome obligation that lasts into late spring.

- Go ahead and use opaque tubs to store your Christmas decorations. You never need to retrieve something from your Christmas tub in July—everything comes out at one time—so it doesn't help to see inside year-round.

- Let your growing supply of tubs serve as a visual reminder to limit your seasonal decorations. Once your supplies don't fit in your tubs (or your tubs don't fit on your one Christmas shelf), you will know it is time to winnow.

- Buy tubs that are small enough to fit on your shelf (no storing tubs on the floor), and make sure they aren't too large to handle or carry.

- Reconsider Christmas cards and gifts. The ever-expanding Christmas gift list (teachers, secretaries, etc.) can make gift giving a burden. Restrict your gift giving to your immediate family. Inform the rest of your list that you are no longer exchanging gifts, and instead send a single donation to a favorite charity to express your gratitude.

Tool Trouble

PROBLEM

"My husband has some shelves in the garage for his tools, but he leaves them out while he is working on a project, which makes a big mess."

SOLUTION

Shelves are fine for storing tools, but it is inefficient to store them separately from where you use them, and your husband understands that he will *never* complete his projects if he has to retrieve and put away tools every time he goes to work on them. What your husband needs is a basement workbench. Clear out an area in the basement so your husband has enough space to both store his tools and work on his projects. Choose a workbench that comes with a Peg-Board for hanging tools and a sliding under-tray on which to set them.

Some utility shelves and a workbench will keep handyman projects off the kitchen table. The peg board and sliding cork-lined tray provide easy access and storage while keeping tools visible.

This shelving unit has built-in open bins for sorting hardware. A supplementary open-bin tray, for the smallest hardware—screws, nuts, and bolts—provides easy access and storage. The unobstructed view enables one to weigh all the inventory and options in a single glance.

Avoid boxes with drawers for tool storage; they allow you to keep too many tools, and you can never tell which tool is in what drawer without wasting time on labels.

Avoid storing your nuts, bolts, screws, etc., in boxes of little drawers—you soon forget what you have in which drawer. Instead, buy open trays with bins that allow you to see all of your small hardware at once, or employ those specialized utility shelves in which the bins are built in.

Adding a Workbench the Easy Way

Basement workbenches need to be assembled, and this just may be too big a project for someone with ADD. Paying to have the store assemble your workbench may well be the most prudent use of your resources. Get this project completed in four easy steps over three or four days:

- Shop for a workbench
- Choose a bench and arrange for delivery/assembly
- Clear a space in your basement for the bench
- Load your tools and supplies onto the bench

The Overstuffed Garage

PROBLEM

"I have three very active young boys. We have so much athletic equipment in our garage that the cars no longer fit. I've been thinking of installing one of those garage storage systems, but they are so expensive."

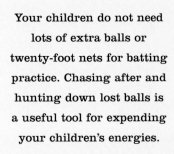

Your children do not need lots of extra balls or twenty-foot nets for batting practice. Chasing after and hunting down lost balls is a useful tool for expending your children's energies.

SOLUTION

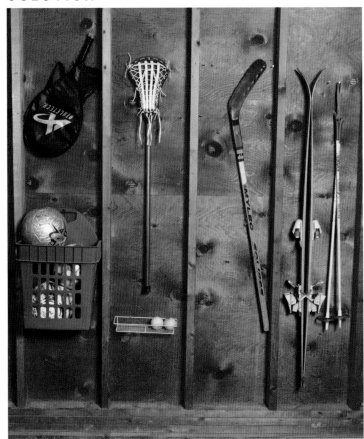

A hamper to hold larger balls is nailed to the wall. The wire shelf from a spice rack holds smaller balls. Athletic equipment is hung from a single nail or supported between two nails.

There is no need for a fancy system; almost any garage can be organized with a hammer, nails, some shelving, and a Dumpster. And there is no expensive system in the world that will allow you to break the laws of physics by cramming more volume into your garage than its dimensions will allow. (And frankly, I just don't see your hyperactive sons disassembling their nets and toys to fit them into complicated and crowded storage systems.) Reduce the volume and number of your athletic gear to an amount that will comfortably fit on your walls and one or two modular shelves.

Hang up as much as possible; cull your athletic equipment down to the versatile essentials, such as balls, bats, rackets, and cones; get it all up on the walls and shelves; and you just may make room in your garage for the car as well as the toys.

It is inefficient to switch items from the garage to the basement for seasonal storage. Whittle your possessions down so that both the skis and boogie boards can live in the garage full-time.

As long as you *limit* your bulk shopping (a twelve pack of paper towels and a case of soda, for example) to a shelf or two on a bank of shelves located between the car and the door to the house, you will have achieved an efficient system for staging dry goods on their way into the home.

Sporting Gear Solutions

GEAR	WHERE TO STORE IT
Basketballs and soccer balls	Inside a hamper nailed to the garage wall
Tennis and lacrosse balls	On a small wire shelf (from a spice rack)
Golf clubs and tennis rackets	Hung from nails or hooks
Bicycle helmets	Hung from the handlebars of the owner's bike
Rollerblade helmets	Dumped on a shelf next to the rollerblades and pads

Organizing Your Garage Space

- Like the basement, the garage space can be organized by employing two or three plastic modular utility shelves and some hooks (or a hammer and nails). This will help eliminate the sense of clutter and help you maintain your space.

- If your garage has cement walls, pay a handyman to install a grid of 2x4s on all three walls. Once the 2x4s are in place, you can use a hammer and nails or some hooks to create a flexible and cheap system for storing the bulk of the possessions you keep in the garage.

- Name each individual utility shelf or bank of shelves. For example, you might designate two shelves on one unit for auto support—ice melt, windshield wiper fluid, and oil will be kept here. (Jumper cables can be hung from a nearby nail.) Designate the other three shelves on this unit to bulk shopping.

- Reduce your inventory in each category so that each category takes up no more than three shelves.

- Leave one shelf on one unit free for use as a staging area in your garage. Sometimes you just need a spot to set down a project or stash an item that is in transit; keeping these objects off the floor and on your staging area will ensure that your garage doesn't deteriorate.

Landscaping and Gardening Equipment

PROBLEM

We have a one-car garage that will barely fit my ADD husband's riding mower, snow-blower, and all of his other landscaping equipment; some of it now needs maintenance, and most of it is almost never used."

SOLUTION

Get rid of the tractor-trailer mower, the snowblower, the leaf blower, rototiller, weed-whacker, and electric hedge trimmers and hire a lawn and plow service instead. You definitely don't have the room to store all of this equipment, and if your husband is maintaining your landscaping, he will continue to impulsively and enthusiastically invest in better and bigger machinery in which he will soon lose interest and then neglect to maintain. Your other choice is to build a second garage bay to house all of this equipment, but wouldn't a lawn service be cheaper?

Families with ADD are almost always better off with a lawn and plow service. But even so, most families will need to maintain some gardening equipment. Reduce your equipment down to a size and number that will comfortably fit in your garage (one shelving unit should be enough to handle all of your gardening and landscape needs), and down to a style that doesn't require maintenance. A simple rake, for example, is easier to store and maintain than a leaf blower, and a shovel will clear snow and can easily be stored on a wall, unlike a snowblower.

Procure simple tools, hang them next to a designated gardening supply shelf, and confine your gardening supplies to only those possessions that will fit on this shelf, and you will have created an efficient and easily maintainable gardening/landscaping center.

Landscaping Equipment Storage Tips

- Although it is nice to have a Peg-Board for long-handled tools, it is not strictly necessary; a spading fork can be hung by its handle from a nail, and a shovel can be hung by resting its head between two nails.

- A flowerpot, with some sand on the bottom for stability, makes an easy "jar" in which to dump your trowel and other short-handled tools, and other flowerpots can be drafted for holding gardening gloves, twine, or other smaller items.

- An open tub on a lower shelf can hold grass seed or potting soil and corral any leakage.

Tools are hung from nails, a flowerpot holds short handled tools, and a lidless tub keeps plastic bags of potting soil from leaking onto the floor.

CHAPTER 12

Packing and Moving

Packing up for a move—or even packing for a trip—can be an organizational challenge for anyone. For those with ADD, who tend to rely on ritual and routine to keep organized, the disruption can be crippling. The only way to minimize the damage is to commit to efficiency while throwing frugality, micromanagement, and over-preparedness out the window. Keep packing simple and brief, and your traveling and moving experiences will be manageable and (relatively) stress free.

Managing a Move

PROBLEM

"I have mere weeks to pack and move, but I'm pretty disorganized. Should I make a list of my stuff? How can I organize this so that I can find everything after we move?"

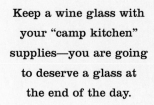

Keep a wine glass with your "camp kitchen" supplies—you are going to deserve a glass at the end of the day.

SOLUTION

Break your moving process down into small, simple, and only necessary steps. Making a list of your stuff is an unnecessary step.

1 Separate out enough clothes and toiletries for seven days, some laundry detergent, and two bath towels per person.

2 In the kitchen, put aside a small subset of dishes and cookware: one pot, one pan, one bowl, one serving spoon, and one spatula; plus one plate, cereal bowl, knife, fork, spoon, and glass per person. Also put aside two dishtowels, a sponge, and some dishwashing liquid. From here on in, consider that you are camping in your own home and that these alone are the items at your disposal. Once your suitcase, toiletries, and "camp kitchen" are set aside, *everything else* can be packed.

3 Begin packing boxes. Fill and label them by designating one box per storage space wherever possible. For instance, one box might have all of the contents of your top bureau drawer and is then labeled—with a quick scrawl in marker—"top bureau drawer." The next box is labeled "second to top bureau drawer." Do not worry if boxes don't fill; it is more efficient to move half-empty boxes and be able to immediately locate your stuff than to pack the boxes efficiently but then have to deal with a confusing jumble of stuff in each box.

4 The day before the move, go around with colored stickers—one for each new room—and mark all of the boxes and furniture. Perhaps blue for the bedroom, red for the kitchen, yellow for the living room. This job should take less than an hour.

5 On the day of the move, tape up a sheet of construction paper in every room of your new home—blue in the bedroom, etc. This way, the movers will deposit all of your possessions in the correct location, and the boxes themselves will be labeled in a way that allows you to immediately find anything you need.

Alternatively, you can call a service that will both pack and unpack the entire contents of your home for you. Depending on your stress level and finances, this may be your best course of action.

It is always best, when moving, to rent a Dumpster to help clear out the old, broken, and unwanted. If you live on a busy street, a "free" sign can also be invaluable.

Leaving Things Behind

PROBLEM

"I travel often on business, but I hate to pack, and I always seem to leave something behind."

SOLUTION

These clear zippered bags—one for hair care, one for medicines and toiletries—are left packed between trips. A supplementary bottle of any regularly prescribed medication is tucked in with the toiletries.

If you learn to reduce the number of items you must assemble, the amount of energy you spend planning, the number of bags you carry, and the volume of items you bring with you, packing will become a less intimidating and stressful job. The three things that contribute most to easy packing are leaving items packed, creating a packing list, and under-packing.

Tips for Effective Trip Packing

- It is inefficient to start every packing job from scratch. Reduce the number of steps and materials by leaving some items packed in your suitcase between trips. A completely assembled toiletry kit—clear so that the contents are always visible—should just live in your suitcase. A duplicate bottle of your regular prescription medicines or even episodic medications that you take only during "flare-ups" should be included in this toiletry bag. By the same token, procure a duplicate sweater or shower shoes—in fact any item with which you always travel—and leave it in your suitcase.

- Create a packing list. If you have a computer, it is worth making a master packing list and leaving that document "open" for a few days so that you can add items to the list as they occur to you. This list should outline everything you need, not just for your business trip but for your beach and ski vacations as well. You can always cross out those things on the master list that are inappropriate for the trip at hand. Bring the list with you so that you don't forget to bring anything back home.

- Under-pack. Under-packing is your friend. You never need more than one suitcase and one carry-on—anything more is likely to get lost. Pack only enough outfits to get you through your trip—no extras, no options, and no "just in case." It is better to occasionally improvise or shop than to constantly carry around enough stuff to see you through every contingency from Hurricane Ivan to dinner at the White House. You can and should pack an extra set of underwear and socks because they are small and pack easily.

It is better to occasionally improvise or shop than to constantly carry around enough stuff to see you through every contingency from Hurricane Ivan to dinner at the White House.

There is nothing more satisfying than exceeding your own expectations. Too often, people with ADD are so frustrated—especially in the realm of organizing—to the point where they actually begin to believe that they can't get organized. I hope that reading this book has given you a renewed sense of confidence that you can accomplish what before seemed impossible, and that barriers to organization are only a problem when you don't have the tricks to avoid them or the tools to conquer them.

In teaching you to challenge and question some of the values and precepts of our modern society and its relationship to "stuff," and by offering a variety of organizing tricks of the trade, I have given you a frame of reference for how to organize, a knowledge base of organizing tools, and a sustainable ADD organizing method. All you have to do is apply this newfound knowledge in short, manageable time intervals to your kitchen cabinets, your bedroom closet, and wherever else clutter lurks. As you continue your organizational projects, I urge you to always ask yourself: Is it quick? Is it simple? Is it efficient? Is it sufficiently reduced?

I wish you good luck—may garbage pick-up always be on the morrow, good health—may all of your groceries be fresh, and good speed—may your calendar stay clear, for all of your organizing adventures!

Acknowledgments

As with all endeavors, a book takes the help and support of many. I would like to thank my editors, Aimee Chase and Wendy Gardner, and all the staff at Fair Winds Press, whose collaboration made writing this book not a chore, but a pleasure. I am indebted to my mentor, colleague, and friend Kathy Waddill, author of *The Organizing Sourcebook,* past president of NAPO San Francisco Chapter, founder of NEPO, and recipient of the President's Award, who motivated, guided, and inspired me in every way. I would also like to express my great appreciation to Julie Jankelson, M.D., Jane Kontoff of ABRHS SPEDPAC, and A. Susan Feeney, A.R.N.P, for sharing their extensive knowledge of ADD, and for giving me unstinting access to their ready ears and quick minds while we processed so many challenges. A very special thank you must go to my dear friend Kristin Leary, whose business acumen and support were so seminal to my early endeavors, and whose unflagging faith and encouragement gave me the confidence to find my vocation. To my clients who opened their homes and their lives, I thank you for the precious trust that allowed me to share your organizational journeys. And of course, none of this would have been possible without the support of my family; thank you to my husband David Pinsky and my mother Marcia Waters, who took care of the home front evenings and weekends while I communed with the computer, and to my daughters Hannah and Leah, whose maturity, generosity, flexibility, and self-reliance gave me the space to create. And finally, a heartfelt thank you to my daughter Esther, who edited my work, both on the book and in life, and whose courage and character in the face of challenge was the inspiration for everything that followed.

About the Author

Susan C. Pinsky is a professional organizer specializing in clients with ADD. She is a graduate of Wellesley College and currently lives in Acton, Massachusetts, with her husband and three children.

Also from Fair Winds

10-Minute Clutter Control Room by Room
By Skye Alexander
ISBN-13: 978-1-59233-145-1
ISBN-10: 1-59233-145-9
$12.00/£7.99$16.95 CAN
Paperback; 256 pages
Available wherever books are sold.

Has clutter taken over your home, your office—your life? You trip over empty shampoo bottles in the shower. Your kitchen looks like the scene of a fraternity food fight. You haven't paid the bills for three months because you can't find them. Break the cycle now and conquer clutter once and for all with the 400 ingenious tips, tricks, and techniques in *Clutter Control Room by Room*.

10-Minute Organizing
By Sara Lavieri Hunter
ISBN-13: 978-1-59233-181-9
ISBN-10: 1-59233-181-5
Paperback; 256 pages
$12.00/£6.99$17.00 CAN
Available wherever books are sold.

If you are you about to give up the battle you've forged to once-and-for-all organize your home—don't. Help has arrived. Your dream of an organized house can become reality, and it doesn't take a lot of time or money. Inside, you'll find 400 simple but ingenious ways to get (and keep) your house organized in just ten minutes—less than the time it takes you to find those misplaced keys!

The Beverly Hills Organizer's Home Organizing Bible
By Linda Koopersmith
ISBN-13: 978-1-59233-154-3
ISBN-10: 1-59233-154-8
Paperback; 192 pages
Available wherever books are sold.

What if organizing your home was as easy as opening a cookbook? With *The Beverly Hills Organizer's Home Organizing Bible*, it is! Like following a recipe, everything you need to organize any part of your home is shown in a clear, easy-to-follow format. For each area, you'll find a list of best tools for the task, how long it will take you, step-by-step directions, and color photos of each step. No more guessing—and no more failures! Whether you need to make more space in a drawer, get that black hole under the sink in shape, or create functional office or attic space, Linda Koopersmith, the organizational expert on the Style Network's hit series, *Clean House*, knows what to do—and shares her professional secrets with you.